D0081570

Planting Hatred, Sowing Pain

Planting Hatred, Sowing Pain

THE PSYCHOLOGY OF THE ISRAELI–PALESTINIAN CONFLICT

Moises F. Salinas

Westport, Connecticut
London

Library of Congress Cataloging-in-Publication Data

Salinas, Moises F., 1966–
    Planting hatred, sowing pain : the psychology of the Israeli-Palestinian conflict / Moises F. Salinas.
      p. cm.
    Includes bibliographical references and index.
    ISBN-13: 978–0–275–99005–3 (alk. paper)
    ISBN-10: 0–275–99005–2 (alk. paper)
1. Arab-Israeli conflict—1993—Psychological aspects. 2. Arab-Israeli conflict—1993—Public opinion.
3. Jews—Israel—Interviews. 4. Jews—Israel—Attitudes. 5. Palestinian Arabs—Interviews. 6. Palestinian
Arabs—Attitudes. 7. Public opinion—Israel. 8. Public opinion—Gaza Strip. 9. Public opinion—
West Bank. 10. Israel—Ethnic relations—Psychological aspects I. Title.
DS119.7.S336483 2007
956.9405′4—dc22   2007003044

British Library Cataloguing in Publication Data is available.

Library of Congress Catalog Card Number: 2007003044
ISBN-13: 978–0–275–99005–3
ISBN-10: 0–275–99005–2

First published in 2007

Praeger Publishers, 88 Post Road West, Westport, CT 06881
An imprint of Greenwood Publishing Group, Inc.
www.praeger.com

Printed in the United States of America

The paper used in this book complies with the
Permanent Paper Standard issued by the National
Information Standards Organization (Z39.48-1984).

10 9 8 7 6 5 4 3 2 1

DEDICATION

To my Family, my wife Jackie, my sons Iky and Danny, and my daughter Ariela. You came with me around the world. I love you.

To all the victims of this senseless conflict and their families. With the hope that your sacrifice will bring one day peace to all.

CONTENTS

ACKNOWLEDGMENTS

When an academic author writes a book, he or she hopes that it will have a positive impact on the world. Less considered is the fact that a book will always have an impact on the author, and that part of the impact is possible only because of all the people that through their direct and indirect help made the writing of a work possible. First and foremost, I would like to thank my two research assistants, Itzik Batito and Alina Manovitz, both students at the Emek Yezreel College, who helped me organize and manage the monumental task of carrying out hundreds of interviews with Israelis and Palestinians. You did a great job, and I am sure that you will have a bright future ahead! I also want to thank all of my students at Emek Yezreel College and Tel Aviv University, who carried out all of these fascinating interviews. Just reading them was an amazing learning experience for me, and I hope doing them was one for all of you too. I want to thank Professor Aliza Shenhar, president of the Emek Yezreel College, who supported me and lent a hand to allow me to use its students, resources, and facilities. Professors Yeshayahu Tadmor, chair of the behavioral science department at Emek Yezreel, Michal Palgi, chair of the sociology department at Emek Yezreel, and Moshe Israelashvili, chair of the Department of Developmental Perspectives of Education at Tel Aviv University, for all their academic and logistic support. Also, thanks to Mohammad Darawshe, from the Abraham Fund, who helped me with access to Palestinian resources and interviewees.

There were many people at my own institution, Central Connecticut State University, who were of tremendous help. President Robert Aebersold and Dean Susan Pease, who supported my sabbatical project against all odds, and my department chair and assistant chair, Dr. Frank Donis and Dr. Brad Waite, who had to suffer without anybody to teach my classes and helped me carry out this project. My gratitude also to Dr. Carol Austad and Dr. Ghassan El-Eid who reviewed and made excellent suggestions to the manuscript. And the Connecticut State University American Association of University Professors (CSU-AAUP) grant committee, who honored me by providing the grant that supported part of this project.

To my friends, Benny Levy and Mike Kagan, who also helped me review parts of the manuscript, thank you for being so annoying and keeping me real! And finally, most importantly, to my Family, my wife, Jackie, and my children, Iky, Danny, and Ariela, who made a tremendous sacrifice. They came with me all the way around the world, leaving their friends, their job, and their school for one year, and stuck with me through three weeks of war even though everybody abroad was calling daily and asking us to leave, all so I could just finish the last of the interviews. To you, my love and my admiration. Thank you.

And to my readers, thank you for taking the time to read this humble work. I hope it also has a small impact on you.

INTRODUCTION

*I don't hate Israelis. All I want, Allah willing, is to have a good life
for me and my children. The problem is, the Israelis are the
obstacle. They are determined to make our life miserable until
we leave or we die. I don't want to give them that satisfaction.*

Hassan, a Palestinian from the outskirts of Jerusalem

*Of course I want peace. All we want is peace. It is the Palestinians
who are the fanatics. They won't rest until they throw us into
the sea.*

Yossi, an Israeli from Tel Aviv

In the Israeli–Palestinian conflict, a bloody conflict that has become a
serious and dangerous struggle that goes far beyond its local ramifications,
the obstacles go way beyond the logical, practical issues of borders and
refugees. These two peoples are caught in a web of irrational behaviors
that sometimes even appear to be against their own interests. For example, in July of 2000, Israeli Prime Minister Ehud Barak, Palestinian
Authority President Yasser Arafat, and U.S. President Bill Clinton met
at Camp David for a diplomatic summit, which was expected to be the
culmination of the long peace process that started with the 1993 Oslo
Agreement. On the eve of the meeting, there were high hopes and expectations, yet the summit failed. Instead of peace, the events ultimately led to
the Al-Aqsa Intifada, a widespread Palestinian uprising. Israel reportedly
followed by a harsh military response, leading to the biggest bloodshed
in the region in decades.

It is evident that neither the Americans, who were on the eve of
national elections at the time, nor the Israelis were willing to stage a major
summit at that point unless the indications were absolutely crystal clear

that a positive outcome was not only possible but highly likely. Therefore, the results of the meeting were not only logically unexpected but also psychologically disappointing. After the failure of the summit, the *New York Times* reported that President Clinton himself felt "exasperated, bewildered, even betrayed"[1] by Arafat, and Madeleine Albright reported that the Israelis also certainly felt betrayed by the failure to reach an agreement.[2]

Why did the process fail? How, if peace was so close and it was clear back then (and even today), that the majority of Israelis accept the idea of an independent Palestinian state[3] and the majority of Palestinians are ready to live side by side with the Jewish state,[4] did the situation deteriorate to the current level of violence, and more than 5,000 people had to lose their lives to fight a war whose goal is at best ambiguous?

Plenty of evidence exists suggesting that both the Israelis and the Palestinians are tired of violence and support efforts to bring about a just and lasting solution to the conflict. For example, the Peace Index, a monthly opinion poll of Israelis' views regarding the conflict and the peace process and carried out by the Steinmetz Center for Peace Research at Tel Aviv University, shows that even during the worst years of the Intifada, 2000–02, the support of the Israelis for the continuation of negotiations and the peace process generally hovered between 50% and 60%. Furthermore, more current Peace Index data from January 2005 show that an astonishing 79.3% of people support the peace process and 54.3% believe that the negotiations will bring about peace in the near future.

Similarly, among Palestinians there are also clear indications of a willingness to end the conflict. For example, a January 2005 poll by the Palestinian Center for Policy and Survey Research (PSR) found that 69% of the Palestinians support a compromise agreement that will end the conflict and recognize both the states of Palestine and Israel. Up to 54% of the Palestinians are willing to support an agreement making compromises in the most contentious issues (i.e., status of Jerusalem and Palestinian refugees) based on a formula similar to the one originally proposed by President Clinton in 2000.

Even in the political arena we can see examples of this contradictory logic that seems to underline the process. For a while, diplomatic developments seemed to go in the right direction to achieve a peace agreement. After the death of Arafat, Mahmud Abbas (Abu Mazen), a pragmatist and a moderate who favors an end to violence, was elected President of the Palestinian Authority. Also, Prime Minister Ariel Sharon of Israel, known as a former hard liner, pushed the Israeli parliament, the Knesset, to vote in favor of an unprecedented step to evacuate all settlements in the Gaza Strip and some isolated settlements in northern Samaria. However, in spite of some concrete gains and possible hope for the future, in practice both Israeli and Palestinian voters seem unable to elect effective leaders and representatives ready for dialogue and real compromise.

There is, therefore, great cause for concern. First, from a purely political point of view, a peace agreement is not nearly as imminent as it was in early 2000. On the other hand, it is true that ongoing surveys by several groups and institutions suggest broad support for a peace agreement. Studies by the Palestinian Central Bureau of Statistics, the Palestinian Center for Policy and Survey Research (PSR), and the Tel Aviv University Center for Peace Studies among others suggest that, in spite of the fact that a sizable opposition still exists, the majority of both peoples agree (or at least are resigned) on the broad parameters of a peace agreement:

- A two-state solution with borders approximating the pre-1967 armistice lines.
- Compensation to all 1948 and 1967 Palestinian refugees, while only a smaller group of them would be allowed to return to Israel proper.
- A joint solution for Jerusalem that will allow both sides to claim some sovereignty.

In practice, however, both governments have eluded any talks about the most contentious issues of Jerusalem, the evacuation and dismantling of major Jewish settlements, and the status of Palestinian refugees, a problematic situation because it is precisely over those issues that the peace efforts can collapse at a political level.*

Moreover, as it was evident at the 2000 Camp David summit, there are even bigger obstacles at the social and psychological levels that might make it extremely difficult to reach an agreement in the near future. The hatred, the stereotypes, and the psychological scars of almost forty years of occupation run deep into the psyche and the social fabric of both the Palestinians and the Israelis. It is clear, therefore, that the solution to

---

*It is important to note that prominent figures on both sides of the conflict have endorsed peace initiatives based precisely on those principles. The Ayalon-Nusseibeh plan, drafted by former PLO representative in Jerusalem and Al-Quds University President Sari Nusseibeh and retired Israel Navy General and member of the Knesset Ami Ayalon, reflects precisely these basic principles. In addition, the Geneva Initiative, proposed by former Israeli minister of justice Yossi Beilin and former Palestinian minister of information Yasser Abed Rabbo, is a detailed document that has the support of many prominent figures on both sides and has received a lot of international backing. See Appendix.

the Israeli–Palestinian conflict cannot be found merely by exploring political solutions to practical problems, which are in and of themselves fairly solvable when compared to the social and psychological difficulties.

If that is the case, then we must look beyond the political hurdles and into the psychological realm if we truly want to understand, and overcome, the obstacles leading to a possible permanent solution. The purpose of this book is to present and explore some of the social and psychological factors that are central to the conflict and its resolution: (1) stereotypes and prejudice, (2) extremism, (3) trauma, and (4) reconciliation.

A Brief Historical Background

In order to better understand the psychological complexities of the Israeli–Palestinian conflict, it is necessary to first look at a little bit of the history of this struggle. Herein, however, lies the first complication, since the *perception* of this history is so different between the two sides, they might as well be talking about two completely separate events. This is not a history book, so I am going to attempt to do a brief narrative, and in order to keep it as objective as possible, I am pulling these accounts from two sources: *A History of Israel* series by Sachar[5] and *Palestine and the Palestinians* by Farsoun and Aruri.[6] I selected these two sources because they are each presented from Jewish and Palestinian perspectives respectively, but at the same time both books try to present a non-biased, objective view of the history of both peoples.

Although some people would argue that the history of Israeli and Palestinian conflict started many thousands of years ago, the history of the modern conflict has its roots at a much more recent time, the end of the nineteenth century. With the emergence of modern nationalism, Jewish emancipation, and civil society in nineteenth-century Europe, many European Jews, who had been the target of centuries of discrimination and anti-Semitism, began to consider the possibility of establishing their own national state in the Land of Israel. At the time, the Land of Israel was called Palestine and was part of the Ottoman Empire. But Israel, and its capital, Jerusalem (or Zion), had been the historic and traditional homeland of the Jewish people, and therefore they established a movement they named Zionism. The most important Zionist leader was Theodore Herzl, an Austro-Hungarian journalist who actually founded the political Zionist movement and called for the First Zionist Congress in

Basle, Switzerland, in 1897. Herzl, and other Zionist leaders, showed very little awareness of the existing Arab population of Palestine at the time, which numbered about half a million people. Many Palestinians were engaged in extensive low-yield agriculture (such as olive orchards) or were shepherds, occupations that require very extensive swaths of lands, which sometimes give the appearance of an "empty" countryside. That explains why Western observers such as the British diplomat James Finn wrote in 1857 that "the country is in a considerable degree empty of inhabitants and therefore its greatest need is that of a body of population."[7] Even famous author Mark Twain[8] had similar observations during his travels through Palestine. For example, about the northern region of the Jezreel Valley, now heavily populated, he wrote: "There is not a solitary village throughout its whole extent—not for thirty miles in either direction. There are two or three small clusters of Bedouin tents, but not a single permanent habitation" (p. 360).

Herzl's writings show that he believed both that Palestine was largely unpopulated and that the few local Arabs would welcome the wealth and modernity that Jewish immigration would bring, while most of the other Zionist leaders at the time either did not consider them a factor or just believed they would integrate into a state of Jews, since they expected several million of the over ten million Jews in Europe would eventually immigrate to the new state. A minority of leaders, however, such as Vladimir Jabotinsky, split from the mainstream Zionist movement, which tended to be socialist and liberal, and formed the "revisionist" wing of Zionism, which actually advocated expelling any Arabs living in the historic territories of the Land of Israel.

At the end of the nineteenth century and beginning of the twentieth, Jews began to emigrate in small numbers to Palestine and established a number of agricultural communities such as Rishon LeTzion, Petah Tikva, and Zichron Yaakov, and later they established the first Jewish city, Tel Aviv, just north of the port of Jaffa. And indeed, at the beginning, the Palestinian population worked in these settlements and welcomed the jobs and the investments. However, that began to change after it became clear that Jews were not looking to come in small numbers but actually attempted to build a whole state for the Jewish people.

A number of events had a major impact on Jewish–Palestinian relationships at the beginning of the twentieth century. First, by the end of World War I, the British took control of the area, which became a British

Mandate. They were a lot more sympathetic to the Jews, who were Europeans after all, than the former Ottoman rulers. Then, in November 1917, the British government issued a letter, known as the Balfour Declaration, which stated Britain's support for the "creation of a Jewish national home in Palestine." This proposal was strongly opposed by Arab leaders, who saw Palestine and Jerusalem as part of the Arab national land that was promised by the British. Indeed, in 1915, Henry McMahon, British High Commissioner in Cairo, had written in a letter to Hussein Ibn Ali, Sherif of Mecca, that "Great Britain is prepared to recognise and support the independence of the Arabs" in most of the Middle East areas, although the letter is quite vague regarding the definition of those boundaries. Nevertheless, these previous commitments of the British, as well as Arab complaints, were ignored by the Britons and the French, who were occupied at dividing the Middle East in areas of influence and did not care much for the native inhabitants.

The British attempted to form joint Jewish-Arab self-governing institutions but failed because Jews were concerned that they would be in the minority and Arabs would not accept having Jews included at all. This failure led to a series of Arab revolts against Jews and against the British mandatory government in the 1920s, led by the Haj Amin El Husseini, a religious leader who later became Grand Mufti of Jerusalem, and Arif El-Arif, a renowned Arab journalist in Palestine. As a response, the Jewish leadership under the command of David Ben-Gurion decided to form a militia called the *Haganah* or "defense."

The riots continued sporadically until they exploded again in 1929. The Palestinian leaders demanded action from the mandatory government. Under pressure, the British government issued a decree to severely restrict Jewish immigration to Palestine. Nevertheless, the Jews continued to immigrate, many of them illegally, to Palestine during the 1930s, driven mostly by the rise of Nazism and anti-Semitism in Europe.

In 1936, a revered Palestinian preacher by the name of Izz al Din El Qassam was killed by the British in a military operation. El Qassam was one of the foremost proponents of the emerging Palestinian nationalism and was seen as a symbol of the Palestinian hopes for self-rule. His death triggered a major uprising that resulted in the deaths of thousands of Jews and Palestinians. Arab leaders demanded once again that the British curtail Jewish immigration, and with World War II looming on the horizon, the British, who did not want to risk losing Arab support at the time, issued severe new restrictions to Jewish immigration, which this time would be much more strictly enforced.

With the beginning of World War II and the Nazi persecution of Jews in Europe, the Jewish leadership in Palestine organized a massive illegal immigration campaign that not only rescued tens of thousands of European Jews but also angered Arab and Palestinian leaders. However, by the end of the war, when it was discovered that about six million Jews were exterminated by the Nazis in what became known as the Holocaust and over one quarter million Jewish refugees were stranded in Europe, international public opinion began to shift in favor of the Jewish establishment in Palestine. The British government, however, was still opposed to opening the doors to Jewish immigration. The Zionist leadership initiated an underground military campaign against the British mandatory forces, originally focusing on damaging infrastructure. However, the most radical right-wing groups that belonged to the revisionist Zionist wing carried out terrorist operations against British military and diplomatic personnel, including the famous bombing of British military headquarters in the King David hotel in Jerusalem, causing the deaths of many dozens of people. Palestinian leaders at the time were also putting pressure on the British to control the Jewish establishment, leaving the British government in an impossible position.

By 1947, because of internal and international pressure, the British turned the official mandate of Palestine over to the United Nations. The United Nations voted in November of that year in favor of a partition plan in which Palestine would be divided roughly in halves, one for a Palestinian state and one for a Jewish one. The partition plan was reluctantly accepted by the Jewish leadership but outright rejected by the Arab governments and the Palestinian population, who saw all of Palestine as their rightful land and did not understand why half of it should be given to the Jews. Making matters worse, at the time there were only about 600,000 Jews in Palestine but over a million Palestinians, making it even harder for them to understand the 50–50 partition. Hostilities exploded between Jews and Palestinians, and there were numerous attacks from both sides on civilian targets, which culminated in the massacre of Deir Yassin by the Jews, in which between 100 and 120 people were murdered, and the massacre of Gush Etzion by the Palestinians, in which about 130 people were killed.

The Arab league and the Palestinians under the leadership of the then exiled Haj Amin El Husseini declared the plan totally unacceptable and warned that if implemented, they would go to war to expel the Jews from Palestine. However, in reality, the Arab governments were far from united, had divergent agendas, and had no strategic coordination whatsoever. In May of 1948 the British Mandate formally ended, and as soon as the British troops withdrew from Palestine, David Ben-Gurion, then formally Prime Minister of the new State of Israel, declared independence, and the Arab governments declared war.

1948: The Independence and the Nakba

The Arab armies initiated a massive attack against Israel, and at the beginning, inflicted heavy damage on the Jewish forces. However, although the Israeli forces were outmanned and outgunned, they were much better prepared and organized than the Arab armies and the irregular Palestinian forces, and soon they were able to turn the tide and repel the initial attacks. There is much controversy surrounding the question whether the Israelis had planned from the beginning to expel the Palestinian inhabitants from the territory that was to become Israel, and the evidence is contradictory. In some cases, like the towns of Lod and Ramla in central Israel, the Palestinian population was certainly evacuated by the Israelis. However, while some evidence shows that officers looked at it as a temporary evacuation to avoid both Palestinian civilian casualties and paramilitary retaliations during the military operations, other historians point at evidence that suggests that it was planned as a permanent expulsion. What is really clear is that about 700,000 people, the majority of the Palestinians, whether by force, at the behest of Israeli forces, or voluntarily, fled or were forced out of the Israeli areas of Palestine during the period of the war of independence, creating for the first time the problem of the refugees, an event the Palestinians call the "Nakba" or disaster.

By the end of the war, Israel held 78% of the territory west of the Jordan River, much more than it was originally allotted by the UN partition plan. The majority of Arab Palestinians now lived as refugees under the rule of the surrounding Arab countries, while Jordan and Egypt held on to whatever was left of their designated state, making absolutely no attempt to promote self-rule or create an autonomous state in those areas. Most of the Arab states who absorbed Palestinian refugees refused to allow them to integrate in their societies, placing them in permanent refugee camps. In addition, a similar number of Jews who lived in those states had to flee these countries as refugees, and many emigrated to Israel, effectively doubling Israel's Jewish population. The Arab states signed an armistice agreement with Israel but refused to recognize its right to exist and therefore did not sign a peace agreement at the time.

The Period After the 1948 War

With no peace agreement and no solution for the problem of refugees, tension between Israel and the Arab states continued to be high. Guerrilla attacks against Israel were commonplace, and in 1956, Israel, with the support of Britain and France, carried out a major preemptive attack on Egypt, conquering the Sinai Peninsula, but later withdrawing under American pressure. The Palestinians, however, were largely ignored both by Israel, who even refused to officially recognize them as a separate nation, and by the Arab states, who only used them and manipulated them to advance their own interests. Palestinians in the exile, however, began to get organized, and in the late 1950s, Arafat founded the Fatah, the precursor faction of what later would become the PLO (Palestinian Liberation Organization), as an umbrella group fighting for all Palestinians. Arafat began to call for the destruction of Israel and reprimanded the Arab states for their inaction. The PLO began to carry out terrorist attacks against Israel in 1965, which it saw as the only viable alternative to achieve liberation in the face of Arab indifference.

Meanwhile, hostilities escalated between Israel and the Arab neighbors, and in the background of the cold war, military actions between the Soviet-backed Syrians and Egyptians and the American-backed Israelis became more frequent. This situation exploded in 1967. Arab leaders openly threatened to destroy Israel, and the combined Arab armies of Egypt, Jordan, Iraq, Syria, and Lebanon began preparations and troop movements. Egypt blockaded important waterways to Israel. Finally, in order to break the blockade and avoid an organized Arab attack, Israel decided to launch a preemptive strike against the Arab forces, dealing them a massive defeat in what was later known as the Six-Day War. In the process, however, Israel occupied the remaining areas west of the Jordan River, as well as the Gaza Strip, the Sinai Peninsula, and the Golan Heights, a fact that instantly placed over one million Palestinians under Israeli occupation, exacerbating the problem of the refugees and creating new ones for a population now living under Israeli military rule.

The PLO became at that point a more formal organization recognized by the Arab governments (and eventually by the United Nations) as the legitimate representative of the Palestinians and repeatedly called for the destruction of Israel. Eventually, the PLO would step up terrorist attacks against Israel and Israeli targets both inside and outside of Israel.

On the other hand, Israel, who initially had been ambivalent about the fate of the occupied territories, began shortly after the war to place limited, strategic settlements in these territories. However, over the years, the policy of limited settlements gave way to an ideological current that called for the full settling of the territories, creating a difficult situation in which Israelis under Israeli civil law live in settlements interwoven among Palestinian towns, who live under Israeli military law and have limited rights and mobility. Today, there are about 200,000 Israelis living in the West Bank, among almost 2.5 million Palestinians.

The Psychosocial Aspects of the Conflict

Exploring the conflict and its possible resolution from a psychosocial perspective is not a simple task. Some researchers, like Rouhana and Bar-Tal,[9] describe the Israeli–Palestinian conflict as an "intractable ethnonational" one, that is, one whose inter- and intragroup characteristics are such that it becomes resistant to resolution. Rouhana and Bar-Tal explain that an ethnonational conflict becomes intractable when it has the following characteristics:–

- totality—it has a life or death existential nature;
- protractedness—it lasts for over a generation;
- centrality—group members' preoccupation with the conflict is central to their life and identity;
- violence—it is endemic to the conflict; and
- perception of irreconcilability—members believe there is no possible solution to the conflict because they perceive the other side's demands as threatening and unrealistic.

Furthermore, Rouhana and Bar-Tal claim that Israelis and Palestinians have developed maladaptive societal beliefs, stereotypes, and prejudices, that, although psychologically helpful to cope with the stressful circumstances of the conflict, they also have the effect of perpetuating it.

Another researcher who has suggested that psychological factors are a major obstacle to achieve a solution to the conflict is Okasha.[10] He suggests that the chronic exposure to violence that both Palestinian and Israeli civilians have endured is a source for widespread psychological trauma. He believes that such trauma brings with it other psychological consequences, such as fear, hatred, and mistrust, that make it impossible for both sides to have a rational rapprochement.

To what extent are these psychosocial aspects affecting both cultures and impeding a resolution to the conflict? Are Israeli and Palestinian cultural and educational streams indicative of stereotypes, prejudices, and hatred that make a political solution more difficult, even unlikely?

The Israelis

After a recent trip to my mechanic, an Israeli Arab from the town of Kefar Kassem, I had a conversation with some of my Jewish Israeli friends about the great service I receive at their garage. Kefar Kassem is an Israeli Arab town, which means that the people who live there are Palestinian Arabs who have Israeli citizenship and have lived in Israel proper since its independence in 1948. I love their service because Arabs are well known for their great hosting skills, and every trip to the garage becomes an experience in which I end up spending lengths of time drinking tea, munching on *baklawah,* and having long conversations with my mechanic and his brothers. However, and in spite of the fact that Kefar Kassem has not experienced any anti-Jewish violence since the beginning of the Intifada (the week it started, there were some demonstrations that turned violent and some property was damaged, but no Israelis were hurt), my Israeli friends could not help but express great concern for my trips to the town. "Aren't you afraid?" they asked. "We would never dare to go down there...it is not only that they don't like Jews, but also the crime level, and the fact that they might be cheating you..." were some of their comments, fueled, mainly, by the social stereotypes of Arabs as violent, treacherous, and deceitful.

To be fair, Kefar Kassem is a place with a lot of infamous history. Ironically, however, this violence has been directed not against Israeli Jews but actually against its Arab inhabitants. In 1956, on the eve of the Sinai war against Egypt, about fifty villagers were killed by Israeli border police because of an unfortunate series of mistakes and an illegal order by a field commander. Although the main commanders responsible stood trials and were sentenced to lengthy jail terms, in reality they served only a small portion of their sentences and were released. Arab villagers remember that dark day still with pain and resentment.

That said, Kefar Kassem is actually a peaceful and rather safe place (as any other in Israel), and I am skilled enough in auto mechanics to be fairly certain that their work has been good, at a very fair price. Unfortunately, my Israeli friends' perceptions of the place are more based on their stereotypes of Arabs and Palestinians, which are seen as violent and criminal, and not on their in-depth knowledge or direct contact with them.

My story illustrates one of the great dilemmas of modern Israeli society. Israel is a democratic country with a strong and aggressive free press and a large percentage of its population that believes in humanistic, egalitarian values. Nevertheless, not unlike other Western democracies (e.g., the United States), it does suffer from a number of cultural stereotypes, not only of Palestinians and Arabs, but also about its own Jewish subcultures. Differently from the United States, however, Israel displays more of the overt, open forms of stereotypes,[11] while in other Western countries, we have seen a shift to the more covert, subtle form of stereotype that psychologists Samuel Gaertner and John Dovidio call "Aversive Racism."[12] Let us review this concept a little bit more in detail. Gaertner and Dovidio suggest that in the past few decades, as open expressions of racism become less tolerated by Western societies and political correctness becomes more dominant, we see fewer and fewer people willing to overtly express the feelings that underlie prejudice and discrimination. They claim, however, that the reduction in the expression of prejudice does not mean a reduction in the feeling of prejudice and that, in fact, prejudice and discrimination have taken a more subtle, covert form of contemporary prejudice, which they call "aversive racism."

Because of the "intractable" nature of the active conflict between Israelis and Palestinians, stereotypes and prejudice of Arabs in general and Palestinians in particular tend to be more open and therefore associated with the classical form of prejudice, as opposed to the aversive racism that has become more typical of Western culture. For example, in one study by First,[13] in which he analyzed the portrayal of Arabs on the Israeli news, he found that in general, content was negatively biased and that Arabs and

Palestinians tended to be underrepresented in the news coverage, and when portrayed, usually identified in "oppositional" activities that confirmed the social stereotypes, such as perpetrators in crime or terrorism stories.

Arabs and Palestinians have also been stigmatized in Israeli culture for a long time in a variety of media. A study by Urian,[14] for example, concluded that theaters in Israel have represented Palestinians in a negative stereotype since the 1970s. Even in plays that were supposed to be sympathetic to Palestinians, they tended to be portrayed as humiliated, exploited, or socially deprived. In another example, Palestinians have also been heavily stigmatized in Israeli filmography. Shohat[15] suggests that through the early stages of Israeli culture, Arabs were presented in a stereotypical and stigmatized manner that presented them as hostile. Even though after the 1980s, Israeli films became more empathetic of Palestinian suffering and were willing to acknowledge their struggle, they still tended to be somewhat biased by a Zionist narrative.

Finally, and more germane to the purpose of this book, Arab and Palestinian stereotypes persisted through the 1990s in educational materials, despite the strengthening of the peace process and the Oslo accord. For example, Surkes[16] reports a study by Daniel Bar-Tal, which suggests, in a content review of over one hundred officially approved Israeli textbooks, that Israeli educational materials reflected the views of a society at war and that Arabs were still stereotyped as backward and uneducated.

Palestinians

If anything, the situation regarding stereotypes and prejudice is even worse on the Palestinian side. Very few studies have looked at the Jewish and Israeli stereotypes in Palestinian culture specifically. Many more have been conducted that look at both Israeli and Palestinian stereotypes (see In the Beginning: Stereotypes, Prejudice, and Other Misconceptions). However, Jewish stereotypes in Palestinian media and culture are so endemic that there is plenty of evidence of their effect on Palestinian society, even without systematic studies. According to the Middle East Media Research Institute, a Washington and Israel based nonpartisan media watchdog, Palestinian media characterizes Zionism as racist on a regular basis, continually supports claims that deny the scope and sometimes even the existence of the Holocaust, and repeatedly calls for the

destruction of Israel.[17] Furthermore, Palestinians are constantly exposed
to cultural products that espouse classical anti-Semitic ideas. For example,
a television series produced by *Hezbollah,* the south Lebanon Shiite militia group, titled *Al-Shatat.* This series is focused on the old middle-ages
myth of the blood libel (in which Jews need the blood of Christian children for the Passover matzoth). Or the Iranian-produced documentary
Al-Sameri wa Al-Saher, which ties a purported control of Hollywood by
the Jews with the century old *The Protocols of the Elders of Zion,* the infamous classical anti-Semitic work which describes the Jewish conspiracy
for world domination. The Palestinian press is also a constant source of
stereotypes and prejudice. A search on LexisNexis and other international
press databases revealed literally hundreds of items that dehumanize Israeli Jews and support inaccurate generalizations of their society. Regularly,
Israelis are depicted as aggressive, murderers, and criminals, a stereotype
that sometimes is even used by extremists to justify the killing of children,
the elderly, and other innocent people since they all share in these traits.
Just as a few examples, the Palestinian Authority newspaper, *Alhayat Alja-
deeda,* published on November 30, 1997, that "Israel acts according to
the Protocols of the Elders of Zion" and that "the greater Zionist plan . . .
was designed when Herzl along with Weizmann traveled around the
world in order to decide the appropriate location for carrying out this
conspiracy." In another press example of blatant stereotypes, the Palestinian newspaper *Al-Quds* (November 1, 1997) printed that the "Jewish
mentality [is] based on the desire to control everything, and which does
not easily grants others their rights."

Palestinians are also exposed to Jewish and Israeli stereotypes through
their mosques, a very important institution in a culture which is quite
observant. For example, according to the Israeli Intelligence and Terrorism Information Center,[18] Friday mosque sermons (normally broad-
casted live) often "include Islamic-based expressions of anti-Semitism
which dehumanize and de-legitimize the Jewish people." Some of the
expressions that have been reported to be commonplace include calling
the Jews and the Israelis "descendents of apes and pigs" and "a cursed
nation, abominable and infidel" who "seek to pollute the mosques."

In summary, as a people under occupation, Palestinians, for the most
part, express their stereotypes and prejudices against Jews and Israelis
freely and without any of the Western ambiguities that lead to aversive
racism. They obviously feel fully justified, but the constant exposure

and repetition of these prejudices is another obstacle to reconciliation and conflict resolution.

Can Psychology Help?

It is, therefore, quite clear that stereotypes and prejudice, which in turn lead to dehumanization, hatred, and extremism, are an important factor in the worsening (and the solving) of the conflict. Can, therefore, psychology lend a hand to help understand it and perhaps lead to dialogue and reconciliation? One of the main foci of this book is to highlight the role that psychology can play to help overcome some of these cultural and social factors that are impeding progress on the political and diplomatic front.

Each chapter includes dramatic ethnographic interviews that were completed using an innovative methodology to ensure they represent the real voice of the victims of this enduring conflict. In contrast to traditional ethnographic research, in which the "Western" researcher interviews and interprets the conversations with the "non-Western" participant, we designed and carried out the interviews with the help of 250 Palestinian and Jewish Israeli students from Emek Yezreel College and Tel Aviv University. Most interviews were done by a member of the same culture as the interviewee, and in the native language, and were then translated into English also with the help of the local students to make the translations more reflective of the originals. I then selected two representative interviews to include in each chapter, not an easy task since many of the interviews were touching, attention-grabbing and each gave a different angle of the plight of two peoples who deep inside only yearn to have a dignified existence. The interviews you will read in this book were selected because they are, in my view, good examples of what average people think and feel in each of the different areas that each one of the chapters of this book covers.

In addition to the interviews, in each chapter I highlight research that has explored some of the possible issues and solutions. For example, in In the Beginning: Stereotypes, Prejudice, and Other Misconceptions, we will review papers like the 2000 study by Slone, Tarrasch, and Hallis[19] that applied intervention strategies to reduce ethnic stereotypes of Arabs among Israeli children. In Hate: The Psychology of Extremism, Dehumanization, and Violence for instance, we will discuss an intriguing paper by de Mesquita.[20] De Mesquita suggests that terrorism actually increases after government concessions. In this chapter, he proposes a model to manage governmental concessions so they would yield the maximum reduction in terrorism.

Similarly, in the chapter dedicated to trauma and psychological consequences, I review literature that deals with the best strategies to reduce the psychosocial effects of conflict-related violence, such as the study by Wexler, Branski, and Kerem,[21] on the treatment of ill children under the undefined conditions of a widespread conflict (one with an unidentifiable "front" and affecting mostly civilians).

Finally, we close with a chapter on peace, dialogue, and reconciliation. The purpose of the last chapter is to outline the contributions of psychology to a process of rapprochement, negotiation, and conflict resolution. I will review studies such as the paper by Maoz, Bar-On, and Bekerman,[22] in which they propose a model of "planned dialogue" to improve mutual communication and understanding, or an article by Bar-Zion,[23] in which he suggests that the failure of previous rounds of negotiations between Israelis and Palestinians is linked to cultural differences that lead to differentiated approaches, expectations, and styles of communication.

In summary, the final chapter is, in my opinion, the most critical of this book, since it also carries with it a message of hope. In spite of all the violence, of all the prejudices, of all the hatred, there are ways in which we can work toward reconciliation. Even though there are huge psychosocial obstacles to peace and though these obstacles, unlike the political and diplomatic ones, tend to be obviated by negotiators on both sides, through the work of researchers, educators, and grass roots activists we can move in a positive direction that will lay the attitudinal foundation which can make political agreements possible. In short, and at the risk of sounding trite, the ultimate purpose of this book is to show that there is light at the end of the tunnel, we just need to know where to look for it.

Notes

1. Jane Perlez, "Whose Holy Land? Diplomacy; Clinton, After Courting Arafat, Feels Frustrated by Latest Turn," *New York Times*, Sec. A, Col. 4, October 11, 2000, 1, Late Edition—Final, Foreign Desk.

2. Madeleine K. Albright, "Breaking the Cycle of Violence," *Washington Post*, October 15, 2000, B07, Op-ed, Final Edition.

3. S. Gazit, "The Voters' Message: Blame it on Arafat," *Jerusalem Post,* February 4, 2003, 7.

4. See the surveys by the Palestinian Center for Policy and Survey Research (PSR)—http://www.pcpsr.org/; also Khaled Abu Toameh, "Most Palestinians Say They Want to Stop the Violence—Poll," *Jerusalem Post,* March 28, 2003, 2A.

5. Howard Morley Sachar, *A History of Israel* (New York: Knopf, 1998).

6. Samih K. Farsoun and Naseer Hasan Aruri, *Palestine and the Palestinians: A Social and Political History,* 2nd ed. (Boulder, CO: Westview Press, 2006).

7. Report to the Earl of Clarendon, Jerusalem, September 15, 1857, F.O. 78/1294 (Pol. No. 36).

8. M. Twain, *The Innocents Abroad,* reissue edition (1881; New York: Penguin, 1966).

9. Nadim N. Rouhana and Daniel Bar-Tal, "Psychological Dynamics of Intractable Ethnonational Conflicts: The Israeli-Palestinian Case," *American Psychologist* 53, no. 7 (1998): 761–70.

10. Ahmed Okasha, "Psychological Impediments to the Peace Process in the Middle East," *Arab Journal of Psychiatry* 14, no. 2 (2003): 75–81.

11. Ami Pedahzur and Yael Yishai, "Hatred by Hated People: Xenophobia in Israel," *Studies in Conflict and Terrorism* 22, no. 2 (1999): 101–17.

12. Samuel L. Gaertner and John F. Dovidio, "Understanding and Addressing Contemporary Racism: From Aversive Racism to the Common Ingroup Identity Model," *Journal of Social Issues* 61, no. 3 (2005): 615–39.

13. A. Gazette First, "Who is the Enemy? The Portrayal of Arabs in Israeli Television News," *International Communication Gazette* 60, no. 3 (1998): 239–51.

14. Dan Urian, "The Image of the Arab in Israeli Theatre—From Competition to Exploitation (1912–1990)," *Theatre Research International* 17, no. 1 (Spring 1992): 46(9).

15. Ella Shohat, "Anomalies of the National," *Sight & Sound* 1, no. 12, Maps & Dreams Supplement (1992): 20–23

16. Sue Surkes, "Hostile Stereotypes Persist Despite the Peace Process," *Times Educational Supplement,* April 1997, no. 4215: 17.

17. http://www.memri.org.

18. http://www.intelligence.org.il.

19. Michelle Slone, Ricardo Tarrasch, and Dana Hallis, "Ethnic Stereotypic Attitudes Among Israeli Children: Two Intervention Programs," *Merrill-Palmer Quarterly* 46, no. 2 (2000): 370–89.

20. Ethan Bueno de Mesquita, "Conciliation, Counterterrorism, and Patterns of Terrorist Violence," *International Organization* 59, no. 1 (2005): 145–76.

21. Isaiah D. Wexler, David Branski, and Eitan Kerem, "Treatment of Sick Children During Low-Intensity Conflict," *Lancet* 365, no. 9466 (2005): 1778–79.

22. Ifat Maoz, Dan Bar-On, and Zvi Bekerman, "Learning About 'Good Enough' Through 'Bad Enough': A Story of a Planned Dialogue Between Israeli Jews and Palestinians," *Human Relations* 57, no. 9 (2004): 1075–101.

23. Bari Bar-Zion, "Understanding Barriers to Peace: Reflecting on Israeli-Palestinian Economic Negotiations," *Negotiation Journal* 20, no. 3 (2004): 383–400.

Planting Hatred, Sowing Pain

IN THE BEGINNING: STEREOTYPES, PREJUDICE, AND OTHER MISCONCEPTIONS

All stereotypes turn out to be true. This is a horrifying thing about life. All those things you fought against as a youth: you begin to realize they're stereotypes because they're true.

David Paul Cronenberg, Canadian film director

I recall an old episode of the TV show *The Simpsons,* in which the lead character, Homer Simpson, is cheering his old friend Carl, an African American, just before a game of basketball. Homer is excited because he is convinced that having Carl on his team will give them an advantage, even though he has never really seen him play. Carl seems upset and asserts that he is "sick" of people assuming he is good at basketball just because he is African American. Typical of the satirical style of *The Simpsons,* of course, Carl proceeds to slam dunk the ball and even break the board *a la* Michael Jordan. This little scene is perhaps one of the best examples of a stereotype I have seen on TV, not only because the humorous character of the show allows for it to be displayed more openly and transparently, but also because it touches on an important and controversial issue regarding stereotypes: That many times they are actually a reflection of real sociocultural characteristics. Could you argue, therefore, that just because African Americans are better on average than whites at basketball, Homer's assumptions were not really stereotypical? Or more to the point, could you argue that just because the majority of the terrorist acts against Western countries are committed by Arab Muslims, that racial profiling in an airport would not be stereotypical either? In order to answer these questions, we first need to discuss the definition of stereotypes and how is it different from another related term, prejudice.

The Term ''Stereotypes''

In its original meaning, the term stereotype refers to a printing plate, usually made of metal and mounted on a wooden block, used for typesetting. The term was used in a social context for the first time by the American writer and journalist Walter Lippmann, in his 1922 book *Public Opinion*. He adopted the term used in the printing realm because he believed it a proper metaphor for the rigid and oversimplified images people had in their heads regarding social groups. The first recorded scientific study on social stereotypes was performed by S.A. Rice and published in 1926 in the *Journal of Personnel Research*,[1] a simple study in which people were asked to identify personal characteristics of individuals based only on a photograph. The field slowly matured through the late 1920s and early 1930s, until the publication of the classical study by Katz and Braly, *Racial Stereotypes of One Hundred College Students,* in 1933.[2] In their study, college students were asked to identify typical characteristics of different ethnic and religious groups. After that, the expression became a standard term in psychology and social sciences, which over the years exploded into a field that has produced tens of thousands of scientific papers.

Although the definition of stereotypes evolved slowly over the decades, it essentially underwent a major transformation in the 1960s. It went from a simple concept of a "negative generalization of social groups' characteristics," which was usually associated with defective thinking or personality,[3] to a more modern sociocognitive view in which stereotypes are seen as normal processes, which are somewhat automatic and can be totally neutral. One of the most accepted definitions, which we will adhere to for this book, is the definition of stereotypes by Ashmore and Del Boca as "a set of beliefs about the personal attributes of a group of people."[4] In other words, assuming that an individual person has a particular characteristic *because* he or she belongs to a specific group (whether or not this characteristic happens to be true of the person or culturally typical of the group). Assuming, therefore, that *The Simpson's* Carl is a good basketball player *because* he is African American is a stereotype, even if Carl is second only to Michael Jordan, and even if on average, African Americans tend to be better at the sport than whites. Similarly, racial profiling, whether at the airport, at an Israeli check point, or even during a traffic stop in New York City, is stereotypical even if most terrorists are Muslim males, or proportionally, there is more crime carried out by African American males than white Americans.

The Connection with Prejudice

In popular language, stereotypes and prejudice are expressions that are often confused and sometimes even used interchangeably. In psychological research, however, prejudice and stereotypes are very different terms that, although connected, refer to very dissimilar phenomena. If stereotypes have been defined in modern research as cognitive and possibly neutral, prejudice, in general, is seen by most contemporary researchers as *affective* (although sometimes as an attitude, yet others as an emotion). There is wide agreement, however, that prejudice has an emotional charge that is certainly biased (usually negatively) toward a specific group. Nelson[5] suggests a broad definition of prejudice, which bridges most of the contemporary research, as "a biased evaluation of a group, based on real or imaginary characteristics of the group members" (p. 11). In other words, while stereotypes are assumptions about the characteristics of individuals, prejudice are evaluations or emotions (usually negative) toward a group as a whole, because we believe that members of that group have a certain characteristic. For instance, we can have a stereotype of the Jews as "stingy" without necessarily being bigoted. However, if that stereotype turns into a *dislike* or a negative evaluation of the group because of our perception (real or imaginary)* that they are tight-fisted, then we become prejudiced.

The Origin and Effects of Stereotypes

Prejudice, therefore, as well as discrimination, are rooted in stereotypes. And, of course, the dislike, the hatred, and the distrust generated by prejudice are major obstacles to reconciliation and the resolution of conflict. Then, in a resilient vicious circle, the continuation of violence

---

*Just as a note to illustrate the endurance of stereotypes: charity and spending patterns among American Jews would seem to indicate exactly the opposite of this stereotype, yet the stereotype persists. While Jews are only about 2% of the U.S. population, according to *Forbes* magazine, 14 Jewish-specific charities are among America's 200 top charities. In addition, market researchers consider Jews to be among the coveted "demographics" because of their spending patterns.

and conflict becomes fertile ground for the development of stereotypes. It is not surprising, then, that the use of stereotypes and prejudice among both Israelis and Palestinians is widespread. Indeed, the major theories of stereotype development actually predict that the current situation in the Middle East is a ripe mixture for their development. For example, one of the more classical theories of prejudice development, the *Realistic Conflict Theory*,[6] proposed by Turkish-American social psychologist Muzafer Sherif in the 1960s, suggests that prejudice and hostile attitudes between groups arise when there is a real conflict for scarce resources, such as land or water. Another major theory of intergroup relations, the *Social Identity Theory*,[7] proposed by psychologists Henri Tajfel and John Turner, suggests that in order to create a strong in-group identification and social identity, groups will derogate external out-groups by using stereotypes and prejudice and by showing in-group favoritism and out-group discrimination. Both theories strongly support the widespread use of stereotypes and prejudice in the relations between Israelis and Palestinians, first because there is a clear, real conflict for land and resources, but more importantly, because, as their national identities emerged in the last century, having an external out-group to malign helped them create stronger in-group social identification.

Stereotypes begin to develop early under these conditions and become much stronger as the child starts to develop a sense of social identity. Unfortunately, there is an acute lack of research in the area of stereotype development among Palestinian children. However, there are plenty of studies from the Israeli side, and it is fair to assume that the development and prevalence of stereotypes is pretty similar among the Palestinians.

One of the major researchers of the study of stereotypes related to the Israeli–Palestinian conflict is Dr. Daniel Bar-Tal, from Tel Aviv University. He has contributed dozens of articles and books, and more recently, his latest book dealing with the study of stereotypes of Israeli Jews, Arabs, and Palestinians. In one of his earlier studies,[8] Bar-Tal investigated the development of the "Arab" stereotype among Jewish Israeli children. After reviewing a series of studies done in Israel with Jewish and Arab children, Bar-Tal reaches a number of conclusions. First, he explains that "since the word 'Arab' is frequently used in Israel, since Arabs are often seen in the streets and on television, and stereotypes about Arabs are widely spread..." (p. 360) children acquire the concept, and develop a basic stereotype, very early in life, at around the age of two and a half or three. Second, Bar-Tal suggests that this stereotype clearly shows negative connotations, such as an association with violence and criminal behavior also at the very early age of between 3 and 6.

Another, more recent study by Teichman and Zafrir[9] confirmed the basic conclusion suggested by Bar-Tal. The researchers interviewed about 400 Israeli Jewish and Arab children with the use of pictures. They concluded that young children, both Jewish and Arab (in this case 7–8 years old), already have clear out-group stereotypes and in-group favoritism and that as the children get older (11–13 years old), although these concepts get more sophisticated and cognitively complex, they remain equally stereotypical.

The paradox of stereotype development is that while we learn them in early childhood when we are not very cognitively sophisticated, they affect our behavior later in life (as we will discuss below), and those behaviors actually end up strengthening and prolonging the stigma. This fuels the endless cycle of stigma–violence–stigma that sometime seems unsolvable. For example, in another study, Bar-Tal and Labin[10] investigated the effect of terrorist attacks on the Palestinian, Arab, and Jordanian stereotypes of Israeli teenagers. They interviewed 119 adolescents during a peaceful period, then again one day after two terrorist attacks, and finally after a three-month period. During the period of quiet, Israeli adolescents showed a more positive concept of Jordanians (with whom there is a peace treaty) than Arabs in general or Palestinians in particular. Nevertheless, following the terrorist attacks, both attitudes and stereotypic perceptions toward all three groups significantly deteriorated. The researchers suggest that a context of violent events does increase negative stereotypes and attitudes against the Arabs and the Palestinians, and from a developmental perspective, growing up in a context of protracted violence can only strengthen and solidify a generalized sense of stigma and prejudice against the out-group.

The Effects of Stereotypes on Israeli–Palestinian Relations

Stereotypes and prejudice do not only fuel violence and prejudice but also become a major obstacle to dialogue and rapprochement in a number of ways. For instance, they impede dialogue because they make it more difficult for the parties to simply listen to each other and understand each other's arguments, even when the sides finally agree to get together. In a study conducted in 1999, psychologist Eshel[11] interviewed Jewish and Arab ninth grade students who participated in intergroup dialogue encounters. Eshel showed that even after the encounters, participants showed significant in-group bias, and that the dialogue between them had little effect because the preconceptions of the students impede them from being open to other's arguments. In another similar study, researchers Orr, Sagy, and Bar-On[12] interviewed 16-year-old Israeli and Palestinian adolescents. They found that they have a tight sense of in-group identity. However, while the closed in-group identity (and out-group stereotypes) of these Israeli and Palestinian teenagers was useful to help them cope with the negative effects of the conflict, it also inhibited their ability and willingness to open up to dialogue. Furthermore, Orr and her colleagues argue that these social representations make both Israeli and Palestinian youths less likely to compromise and make sacrifices to achieve peace.

In a series of studies published in 2002, Maoz, Ward, and Katz[13] suggest the mutually negative social perceptions of Israelis and Palestinians reduce their willingness to accept peace proposals and bias their judgments about the favorability of such proposals. For example, in one study, Israeli Jews were presented with an actual, though little known, proposal for a peace plan. Half of the Israelis were told that the plan was authored by the Palestinians, while the other half were told the plan was a proposal from the Israeli government. Participants evaluated the proposal less favorably when the plan was attributed to the Palestinians and more favorably when it was attributed to the Israeli government, even though both groups saw the exact same proposal. In a second study, Jews and Arabs were presented with another actual peace plan that in reality has been proposed by the Palestinians. Similar to the first study, both groups evaluated the plan more negatively when it was attributed to the "other side," while Jewish participants that identified with the right wing perceived even the Israeli-ascribed proposal as negative.

In general, stereotypes also prevent us from being able to relate to and be tolerant toward other cultures. Since we evaluate an out-group based on a small number of simplified and generalized characteristics, instead of in a complex way, we develop a basic inability to understand the stigmatized culture's narrative. In an interesting study by Abu-Rabia,[14] he looked at a group of people who would be expected to be more open and tolerant of the other culture: Israeli Arabs learning advanced, elective Hebrew, and Israeli Jews learning elective Arabic. One would expect that second-language students would naturally be more attracted to the culture of the language they seek to learn, right? In his study, Abu-Rabia gave three

Jewish-cultural short stories (by Martin Buber) and three Arab-cultural short stories (by Jamal Jubran) to a group of about 150 Jewish and Arab high school students. The stories were presented to the students in random groups either in their original language or in a language translation. After that, the students were given tests of explicit (i.e., the actual story) and implicit (i.e., more culturally contextual) comprehension. Not surprisingly, students were able to better comprehend the explicit content of the stories when the stories were presented in the native language. However, according to Abu-Rabia, even in the native language, the students found the nonrelated cultural stories pretty much "incomprehensible" at the implicit level. By contrast, a control group of Arab Canadians were much better able to comprehend the nonrelated cultural stories, suggesting that it is *the sociocultural context* of the Israeli–Palestinian reality, that is rife with stereotypes, that is the barrier to cross-cultural understanding, even for students who have elected to learn the other's language.

These results are not surprising, since stereotypes distort our perception and bias our understanding not only of the culture and social situation but also of history. An eerie effect that is reminiscent of George Orwell's *1984* is that the stigma of an out-group affects not only our interpretation of past events but also our outright recollection (and subsequent narrative) of the events, creating in fact two parallel histories that only vaguely resemble each other.

One example of this phenomenon is illustrated in a 2004 study by Porat,[15] in which a group of Israeli high school students were asked about their recollection and interpretation of a 1920s' historical event which is a cornerstone of Israeli Zionist identity: the Tel Hai attack. Tel Hai was an early agricultural settlement in the upper Galilee, which became part of the Israeli historical folklore when one of its leaders, Joseph Trumpeldor, and five of his colleagues were killed during heroic resistance when the settlement was attacked by Arabs. According to the legend, as Trumpeldor agonized, he uttered the words: "Never mind, it's good to die for our country." Recent historical evidence and a more in-depth examination of the records, however, have cast strong doubt on the major aspects of the legendary story.[16] The historical record and available documents show that apparently, the attack by the Arabs was the result of a misunderstanding and not hostility toward the Jewish settlers, as it was originally believed. Instead of heroic resistance, the Jewish settlers promptly fled Tel Hai after the initial armed confrontation and only returned several months later to rebuild it. And finally, it is highly doubtful that Trumpeldor ever uttered his famous last words. In Porat's study, the students were presented with the revisionist, more historically valid view of the Tel Hai events (which is, by the way, the one that is presented in official Israeli textbooks since the 1990s). The participants had extensive opportunity to explore and discuss it with the researchers. Twelve months later, the students were asked their recollections of the Tel Hai event. According to Porat, none of the students who participated adopted the more historically accurate narrative they had reviewed earlier. Students from a more Zionist-Nationalist background ignored the historical narrative entirely and regressed to the purely legendary account of the event. Students from a more liberal background either adopted the legendary narrative in its entirety or combined details from the historical and legendary accounts. In conclusion, the social and cultural background of the Israeli and Zionist context is powerful enough to distort the interpretation of historical events, to fit the in-group enhancing narrative, even after the students had ample opportunity to learn and explore a more historically accurate account.

Another study that exemplifies how the social construction of national identity, and the resulting stereotypes, affects the interpretation of history was performed by Sagy, Adwan, and Kaplan, a joint group of Israeli and Palestinian researchers, in 2002.[17] The researchers wanted to know how the different societies' interpretation of their own and the other's historical narrative affected their expectations of the future. They developed a questionnaire that touched on many important historical events for both peoples but focused on two central events of the Israeli and Palestinian histories: the Jewish Nazi Holocaust and the Palestinian *Al Nakba* (the Disaster), the events surrounding the 1948 Israeli war of independence in which many of them lost their homes. They gave these questionnaires to over 2,000 Israeli and Palestinian high school students and asked them to rate the levels of legitimacy (Is the other side's recount accurate? Is it valid?), as well as their own empathy and anger toward the out-group. Overall, Sagy, Adwan, and Kaplan found that both sides displayed low levels of empathy, unwillingness to accept and legitimize the other side's narrative, and high levels of anger toward the other's perspective. These feelings, consequently, translated into reluctance of either side to acknowledge the other's narrative mostly on the emotional (empathy) but also on the cognitive (accuracy) levels. In addition, Sagy and her colleagues found some low but significant relationships between the delegitimization and the anger toward the other side. They conclude with a bleak forecast for a resolution of the conflict, suggesting that these feelings are indeed a psychological obstacle to a real solution to the struggle.

Stereotypes affect not only our views of culture, society, and history but also our perception of the "other's" present *individual* behaviors. In other words, we are likely to be negatively biased when judging the acts of an individual who belongs to the out-group.

One well-documented consequence of this effect is how we judge differently the seriousness of a crime depending on the race or ethnicity of the alleged offender. Many studies have shown that in the United States, for example, we tend to perceive that a crime is more serious when committed by an African American or a Latino against a white person than vice versa. The same is true in other societies where powerful stigmas exist against minority groups. Hurwitz and Peffley,[18] in an extensive review of the literature, clearly show that when the alleged perpetrator of a crime belongs to a stigmatized minority, people in the majority group tend to perceive *the same crime* as harsher and more serious than if it was committed by a member of the majority. In the United States, where a jury is more likely to be affected by this stereotype bias, it is widely documented that African Americans and Latinos tend to receive harsher sentences for the same crime than whites.[19] The same phenomenon has been studied in Israel by Herzog.[20] He surveyed 620 Jewish Israelis and 315 Israeli Arabs, asking them about the seriousness of a number of crimes that ranked from the relatively minor (e.g., false tax reports and watch theft) to the major (e.g., wife murder and ideological murder). The participants were asked to rank the seriousness of the crimes and told it was committed either by an Arab offender or by a Jewish offender. Although Herzog found no significant differences in the perception of seriousness for most crimes regardless of ethnicity (even the serious ones), he found a very significant difference when the crimes were committed in an interethnic manner, that is, Jewish subjects tended to perceive a crime as more serious if an Arab committed it against a Jew than if one Jew committed it against another Jew, and vice versa. In other words, both Israeli Jews and Arabs consider a murder to be more serious if the murderer was a member of the "out-group," even if the murder scenario is virtually identical, and even if not motivated by ideological or nationalistic factors.

Another study that shows that the judgment of the behavior of Israelis and Palestinians is biased by their mutual stereotypes and prejudice was conducted by Pitner, Astor, and Benbenishty.[21] In this study, they divided about 2,600 Israeli and Palestinian adolescents into four groups.

Each group was presented with a fictitious scenario in which one child insulted another and the other child, in retribution, hit back at the first child. The only difference between groups is that the nationality (Israeli or Palestinian) of the children was changed, and therefore we had four different combinations: Jew against Jew, Palestinian against Palestinian, Jew against Palestinian, and Palestinian against Jew. After that, the adolescents were asked to answer (in a questionnaire) how justified was the second child to hit back the first. Although Pitner and his colleagues found that the adolescent's views were more influenced by the actual scenario than by the stereotypes, still "a large proportion of students in this study stereotyped the other group as more violent" (p. 418), and, consistent with the other studies we have reviewed, were more willing to justify the retribution when the scenario was about somebody from the out-group against a child from their in-group.

To summarize this section, the evidence is clear that when it comes to the behaviors and perceptions of both Israelis and Palestinians, stereotypes cloud their judgment, bias their perception, and prevent them from empathizing with their enemy. However, these might not be the worst consequences of stereotypes, because they might have a stronger, more primal effect that can become an even bigger obstacle to peace: Stereotypes fuel their fear.

Stereotypes, Fear, and Hatred

Fear is a primal emotion that overrides logic. Even when confronted with great opportunity, with wealth, with passion, fear is a great barrier that prevents us from acting. Moreover, fear is a huge negative motivator when it comes to acts of hatred and violence. And certainly, fear, as a cultural phenomenon, is closely tied to stereotypes. Perhaps nobody said it better than British writer and Nobel Prize winner Bertrand Russell in his book *An Outline of Intellectual Rubbish* (1943): "Collective fear stimulates herd instinct, and tends to produce ferocity toward those who are not regarded as members of the herd." And when it comes to the Israeli–Palestinian conflict, this metaphor is in fact supported by theory and research from a psychological perspective. Bar-Tal[22] explains why fear overrides hope in societies engulfed in protracted conflicts. Fear, he explains, is actually an adaptive response to situations of threat and, therefore, a positive emotion in that sense. However, threat is subjective. It can be the result of our own, inaccurate learning about certain situations. Take for instance, Tarantula spiders, which are big and hairy and tend to produce an acute fear reaction in most people because most of us believe their poisonous bite can be deadly. However, Tarantulas, in fact, are not more poisonous than an average bee. Or as the Web site for the California Poison Control System put it: "most bites do not produce any significant poisoning symptoms." The fear we associate with the big, scary Tarantulas is not based on an objective, fact-driven reaction, but rather on an inaccurate, learned and conditioned response that is the result of a cultural misconception, or a "stigma," if you will. We fear these spiders because of the countless horror movies and TV programs in which we have seen them as swift, lethal creatures.

Collective fear in protracted conflict emanates, to a degree, from the same source. Even though two enemy societies might *hope* for peace and wish to end the bloodshed, the conditioned learning that the prolonged conflict has produced generates a primal, conditioned response of fear that can override logical thinking and prevent us from reaching an agreement. Stereotypes fuel fear. They become the source of our conditioned learning, and we learn to associate the enemy with all the negative characteristics of the stigma. Bar-Tal explains that this perceived fear can lead to a number of effects, such as over-sensitization to threatening cues, overestimation of danger, increased expectation of threat, prevention of openness to new ideas, and increase in the likelihood of "defensive" aggression. To search for empirical support and factual examples of this process, Bar-Tal reviews a number of areas in Israeli culture, such as literature, education materials, and the press. He did find numerous examples in which social fear has fueled stereotypical thinking and impeded advancement in the peace process. For example, he refers to many depictions, even among left-leaning Israeli writers such as Amos Oz and A. B. Yehoshua, in which fear and stereotype are connected through depictions of them as "frightening, cruel, inhumane, out to harm, to destroy and kill" (p. 613). He concludes that, in the case of Israel, stereotypes and fear are a major obstacle to the hope for reconciliation and that the collective memories of the Arab–Israeli conflict, together with a much wider history of persecution of the Jewish people, feed the fear and the stereotypes. Nevertheless, Bar-Tal ends with a positive note, emphasizing that it is possible to change from collective fear to collective hope with determination, openness, and creativity, a theme we will come back to in the final chapter of this book.

Finally, by promoting fear and overriding logical thinking and hope, stereotypes fertilize the ground for the mergence of radicalism and hatred. The best way to assuage this fear is with simplistic, strong, and straightforward responses associated with fight or flight responses, and therefore a strong, aggressive stance becomes a lot more popular among societies immersed in protracted conflict than the more logical, but complex and uncertain, view of reconciliation. A number of studies have looked into how stereotypes promote radical thinking in Israeli and Palestinian societies. For example, Rubinstein[23] asked about 820 Jewish Israeli and Muslim Palestinian college students to complete the RWA (Right Wing Authoritarianism) scale. The scale measures a concept first proposed by the prominent psychologist Theodore Adorno in his book, *The Authoritarian Personality*. The RWA was first proposed in relation to German Nazis, and it is closely associated with prejudiced and stereotypical thinking, conservatism, and extremism. Rubinstein found that, in fact, RWA was correlated among both Israelis and Palestinians with support for more aggressive right-wing policies and religiosity, and that it was higher among Palestinians than among Israelis. In another study, Moore and Aweiss[24] gave a questionnaire to over 3,700 Israeli, Israeli Arab, and Palestinian high school students and asked them about their attitudes, their political beliefs, and the hatred for each other. They found that although Palestinians showed less tolerance and openness toward the out-group, in all groups, their attitudes and political beliefs were related to hatred, and that hatred was also related to support for more extreme measures regarding the Israeli–Palestinian conflict. In conclusion, students who have a more negative, stereotypical view of the out-group tend to be more extreme and support more radical positions.

Chapter Conclusion

Stereotypes are only one link in the vicious circle of violence that makes solving the Israeli–Palestinian conflict a difficult proposition. As we have seen, they both fuel and are fueled by fear, by violence, and by extremism. They override logical thinking, and because of their simplicity and their efficiency to judge out-groups, they become the easiest way to relate to an enemy during a protracted conflict. Hope, on the other hand, requires breaking these stereotypes and requires people to be open, flexible, and creative. Hope obliges people to higher, complex, and sophisticated thinking, and therefore, it is harder to find hope than to find fear and stereotypes.

Finally, stereotypes feed extremism, but it is also in the interest of the extremist to nourish the stereotypes because people with stereotypical views are more likely to support radical positions and actions. Their very existence depends on the continuation of the stereotypes and the continuation of the conflict. In our next chapter, therefore, we will explore the complex issues involved in the world of extremism and radicalism.

Notes

1. S.A. Rice, "'Stereotypes': A Source of Error in Judging Human Character," *Journal of Personnel Research* 5 (1926): 267–76.

2. D. Katz and K. Braly, "Racial Stereotypes of One Hundred College Students," *Journal of Abnormal and Social Psychology* 28 (1933): 280–90.

3. T. Adorno and others, *The Authoritarian Personality* (New York: Harper, 1950); A. Maslow, *The Farther Reaches of Human Nature* (New York: Arkana/Penguin Books, 1971).

4. R.D. Ashmore and F.K. Del Boca, "Conceptual Approaches to Stereotypes and Stereotyping," in *Cognitive Processes in Stereotyping and Intergroup Behavior,* ed. D. Hamilton (Hillsdale, NJ: Lawrence Erlbaum, 1981).

5. T.D. Nelson, *The Psychology of Prejudice* (New York: Allyn and Bacon, 2002).

6. H. Tajfel and J. Turner, "An Integrated Theory of Intergroup Conflict," in *The Social Psychology of Intergroup Relations,* ed. W.C. Austin and S. Worchel (Montery, CA: BrooksCole, 1979).

7. H. Tajfel and J. Turner, *An Integrative Theory of Intergroup Conflict. Intergroup Relations: Essential Readings* (Psychology Press, 2001), 94–109.

8. Daniel Bar-Tal, "Development of Social Categories and Stereotypes in Early Childhood: The Case of 'the Arab' Concept Formation, Stereotype and Attitudes by Jewish Children in Israel," *International Journal of Intercultural Relations* 20, no. 3–4 (1996): 341–70.

9. Yona Teichman and Hilla Zafrir, "Images Held by Jewish and Arab Children in Israel of People Representing Their Own and the Other Group," *Journal of Cross-Cultural Psychology* 34, no. 6 (2003): 658–76.

10. Daniel Bar-Tal and Daniela Labin, "The Effect of a Major Event on Stereotyping: Terrorist Attacks in Israel and Israeli Adolescents' Perceptions of Palestinians, Jordanians and Arabs," *European Journal of Social Psychology* 31, no. 3 (2001): 265–80.

11. Yohanan Eshel, "Effects of In-Group Bias on Planned Encounters of Jewish and Arab Youths," *Journal of Social Psychology* 139, no. 6 (1999): 768–83.

12. Emda Orr, Shifra Sagy, and Dan Bar-On, "Social Representations in Use: Israeli-Jewish and Palestinian High School Students Collective Coping and Defense," *Megamot* 42, no. 3 (2003): 412–36.

13. Ifat Maoz, Andrew Ward, and Michael Katz, "Reactive Devaluation of an 'Israeli' Vs. 'Palestinian' Peace Proposal," *Journal of Conflict Resolution* 46, no. 4 (2002): 515–46.

14. Salim Abu-Rabia, "Are We Tolerant Enough to Read Each Other's Culture? Evidence From Three Different Social Contexts," *Educational Psychology* 16, no. 4 (1996): 379–88.

15. Dan A. Porat, "It's Not Written Here, But This Is What Happened: Students' Cultural Comprehension of Textbook Narratives on the Israeli-Arab Conflict," *American Educational Research Journal* 41, no. 4 (2004): 963–96.

16. Y. Zerubavel, "New Beginning, Old Past: The Collective Memory of Pioneering in Israeli Culture," in *New Perspectives on Israeli History,* ed. L.J. Silberstein (New York: New York University Press, 1991), 193–215; Y. Zerubavel, *Recovered Roots: Collective Memory and the Making of Israeli National Tradition* (Chicago, IL: University of Chicago Press, 1995).

17. Shifra Sagy, Sami Adwan, and Avi Kaplan, "Interpretations of the Past and Expectations for the Future Among Israeli and Palestinian Youth," *American Journal of Orthopsychiatry* 72, no. 1 (2002): 26–38.

18. Jon Hurwitz and Mark Peffley, eds., *Perception and Prejudice: Race and Politics in the United States* (New Haven, CT: Yale University Press, 1998).

19. For example, E. Rosenblatt, *Criminal Injustice: Confronting the Prison Crisis* (Boston, MA: South End Press, 1996).

20. Sergio Herzog, "Does the Ethnicity of Offenders in Crime Scenarios Affect Public Perceptions of Crime Seriousness? A Randomized Survey Experiment in Israel," *Social Forces* 82, no. 2 (2003): 757–81.

21. Ronald O. Pitner, Ron Avi Astor, and Rami Benbenishty, "The Effects of Group Stereotypes on Adolescents' Reasoning About Peer Retribution," *Child Development* 74, no. 2 (2003): 413–25.

22. Daniel Bar-Tal, "Why Does Fear Override Hope in Societies Engulfed by Intractable Conflict, As It Does in the Israeli Society?" *Political Psychology* 22, no. 3 (2001): 601–27.

23. Gidi Rubinstein, "Authoritarianism Among Jewish Students in Israel and Palestinian Students in the Occupied Territories," *Megamot* 41, no. 4 (2002): 557–74.

24. Dahlia Moore and Salem Aweiss, "Hatred of 'Others' Among Jewish, Arab, and Palestinian Students in Israel," *Analyses of Social Issues and Public Policy* 2, no. 1 (2002): 151–72.

INTERVIEWS

An Interview with Ana, Who Lives in Tel Aviv. Interviewer: Teren Feldman

Ana is a 20-something Jewish woman from Tel Aviv. She is a student and is not particularly involved in any political group.

Interviewer: Hello Ana.

Ana: Hello.

Interviewer: Why don't you start by telling me something about yourself?

Ana: Well, my name is Ana, I am a student, I am Israeli and I live in Tel Aviv.

Interviewer: Thank you. You know this interview is about the conflict between Israel and the Palestinians. So, can you tell me what is your opinion about the Israeli–Palestinian conflict?

Ana: I think that it is not an issue of who has the right to live here, us or them. From an equal rights point of view, I think that I am in favor of us and not against them. I am simple in our favor. I think that we should live here. This is our land.

Interviewer: Where do you think they should live, then?

Ana: We should have expelled them in 1948. We didn't do it, and it was a mistake and I don't know what to do today. We have to find a solution. I don't know if we should be kicked out or if we should give them a state of their own.

Interviewer: So you don't agree with all the idea of returning territories and peace with the Palestinians?

Ana: We shouldn't return any lands.

Interviewer: What about the "disengagement"?

Ana: The Prime Minister (Sharon) should have asked our opinion before the disengagement, and explain to us what exactly was going to happen and what is the meaning of it from the political and territorial points of view. He did not explain it to us, and therefore I was against the disengagement. Beyond that, I don't think it will solve our problems if they have a state of their own. What is happening now just proves my point. They gave them the opportunity for a state and they go and elect Hamas (the radical Islamic group) to govern them. They are terrorists.

Interviewer: What do you think will happen now that (radical Islamic Movement) Hamas was elected?

Ana: We have to wait and see. They are terrorists. It is their nature, their nature is to kill. We can't do a comparison with the Etzel* of back then or the (right wing) Likud party. They were not murderers and were not in the business of killing Brits in order to kick them out of Israel. They were in the business of scaring them so they would leave. The Hamas are in the business of murdering us. It is us or them. Their flag is a flag with the State of Israel in it. Their flag is green and over it is the State of Israel. Like it is their territory! They will never be content with what we'll give them. Maybe what we will give them as the result of peace will allow them to purchase more weapons and develop themselves militarily. Also because we would not have control there, it will give them just more weapons so later they can try to control all of the country.

Interviewer: So how would you summarize your political views?

Ana: I tend more to be right wing, on the next elections I will vote for a right wing to radical party instead of a center or left wing party.

Interviewer: Why do you think we have not been able to solve the conflict?

Ana: Because we can't solve anything with them because they are Arabs. They are Arabs, their attitude is one of Jihad (Holy War): "We will control the world and everybody will be a Muslim." That is what they are doing in France and it is what they did in Britain, all the riots they had. They are never satisfied with what they get. It is their thing from the Koran that they believe in wars and specially in Jihad war.

Interviewer: When you say "they are Arabs and you can't make peace with them" what do you mean?

Ana: First of all their religion is against peace, Jihad is what they are, what can you do? They are liars by nature, and they are not trustworthy.

---

*The Etzel, Irgun Tzvai Leumi, or the National Military Organization was a right-wing extremist Zionist guerrilla group that operated in the late 1940s and was responsible for the bombing of the King David hotel in Jerusalem as well as the killing of Palestinian civilians.

Even the Arabs we have here across the street (Israeli Arabs) are like that. Just give them half a chance and they will behave like them. I don't like Arabs, I don't trust them. I think that by their nature they don't want peace with us. Look at what happened here in the year 2000, when they started rioting. I don't exactly remember what happened in (the Israeli Arab towns of) Sachnin and Maj'd, over nothing they destroyed the traffic light, they climbed the poles and created a siege on (the Jewish Israeli city of) Karmiel and they kidnapped Jewish people at (the store) Dabach and didn't let them leave. It was a real mess.

Interviewer: Don't you think that if they have their own country all the problems could be solved?

Ana: No, because they would not be interested in peace. They will want to continue the war.

Interviewer: Even if they elect somebody who is not like Hamas or another terrorist organization?

Ana: That would not happen, because we did let them carry elections, and they choose Hamas. That would never happen because they have youth camps of the Hamas Youth where they teach them how to blow up! They are brainwashed from a very early age against Israel.

Interviewer: It is not necessarily everybody. It is only a radical group.

Ana: It is a lot of them. They just had democratic elections and a lot of them voted, and they voted Hamas. That is their message: war and not peace. Everybody knows what is Hamas' message. So, it is true that there are some of them who want peace, but even they don't really want peace. So, it is us or them at the end. There are no choices, so we either give them the country and they can live here, or we don't give them the country and it will be ours and we will fight them over it. So there is no middle ground solution. They too are not willing to have a middle ground solution.

Interviewer: Don't you think that the separation fence can be a possible solution?

Ana: A fence, and not letting them come in, can be a solution only if they are cordoned by it within themselves.

Interviewer: What is your opinion about the support of France and Russia to the Hamas?

Ana: The French have always been against the Jews, and there is nothing to do about that. It is easy to hate the Jews. Everything comes from the hate against the Jews. And from the fact that Israel doesn't market itself properly around the world. All the Arab–Israeli conflict, we don't show the world what the Arabs are really capable of doing. The Palestinians show the rest of the world how miserable they are and that we destroy their homes. Israel should explain why they are demolishing their homes, that [we do it because of] the moment that their son exploded in a bus and killed ten Israelis. I remember that once on CNN they gave thirty seconds to a mother whose son was killed in a terrorist attack, and to the mother of the terrorist they gave like a minute and a half and they described how miserable she was that her son had died, but her son was actually a murderer!

Interviewer: So, do you think that the disengagement helped or hindered Israel's image abroad?

Ana: The disengagement helped with the attitude of the world in relation to Israel. Because the world can see that we are in favor of peace and we are willing to give them land to create their own country.

Interviewer: What do you think will be the solution at the end?

Ana: Generalized war. Which hopefully we will win.

Interviewer: Do you mean a war against the Palestinians or against all the Arab countries around us?

Ana: I think it will be Israel against all the Arab countries. Only after the war all the problems will be solved. I don't think it will be a generalized war only of Israel against the Arabs, but of all the world against the Arab world, and Israel will be involved in it. Israel will not start it, but it will be the point from where the rest of world will go out against the Arabs. For instance, Israel against Bin Laden and al Qaeda is just a small paragraph because they enjoy targeting us. Their main targets are not just Israel but the rest of the world. We are just in the way. The cherry on top of the cake.

Interviewer: Don't you see any other solution outside of generalized war like for instance negotiations?

Ana: I don't think this issue will be solved through negotiations. Other than war, there won't be any other solutions.

Interviewer: Do you think that after war the Israeli–Palestinian conflict will be solved?

Ana: Yes, because either there won't be here any more Arabs or there won't be here any more Jews. In my opinion, the Jews will stay because the Jews have an amazing survival power. We survived the Holocaust, and we will survive them too. Jews were not meant to die, God would not want that. He would want us to survive and continue to eternity. That we will show the rest of the world the ray of light and the right path.

Interviewer: How do you think we could do a total war without sanctions from the world?

Ana: I think Israel will continue to fold and to fold because we don't have the will to do anything, because they (the government) have to do what the world wants. Only that at some point, everybody will go in a war against everybody. Then maybe all the problem will be solved. I think that Israel, today, has no response capacity because they don't allow her to respond the way it's needed. Israel has to wipe them out. Every day there are Qassam rockets falling in (the Israeli city of) Ashkelon and so on. Is it logical? In what country would it be logical that something like that would happen? If it were the United States it would have, long ago, send them nuclear missiles.

Interviewer: Do you think that (Israeli Prime Minister) Sharon would have been able to do that?

Ana: Sharon could not have. None of them would dare do that. Because the Americans are on their back not letting them do it. The disengagement wasn't an anti-Arab program, it was an anti-right-wing program. They kicked Israelis out of their homes, of their workplaces. Without giving them any alternative solutions.

Interviewer: Did you always have such views?

Ana: No, at some point I was in the (Israeli left wing party) Meretz Youth.

Interviewer: What made you change?

Ana: The 2000 riots. I think that what broke the camel's back was the two reservist soldiers that made a wrong turn and by mistake entered (the Palestinian city of) Ramallah, and they just murdered them and after that the Palestinians immersed their hands in their blood like it was some sort of sacred ritual. They all murdered those disgusting Jews. It was horrifying to see that. They behaved toward those people as if they were dirty animals. In addition, there was the story about the Palestinian child that got killed and that later they found that he died from a Palestinian bullet. They showed the world that we supposedly killed him, and they played with the feelings of the rest of the world while they in fact did that themselves. After that I understood that there is nobody to talk to. They are murderers, there is no partner for peace, only a partner for war. So, the quicker we fight the better. The quicker we understand that we need to fight them and give them a painful response for every painful operation they do to us, the better.

Interviewer: What is your opinion about the settlers (in the occupied Palestinian territories)?

Ana: Settlers who cause that soldiers have to go in and beat them, who confront the soldiers, I'm against them. I am a right winger against the settlers.

Interviewer: Anything else you would like to add?

Ana: Yes, the cease fire we have right now is just temporary and has only given them time to rearm. The minute it is over they will attack us. Now even Russia and France will supply them with weapons and ammunition.

An Interview with Soha, Who Lives in Jenin. Interviewers: Daphna Bechar and Einav Chansi

Soha is a Palestinian woman from Jenin, who has a sick child, and needs to cross to Israel periodically to be able to get medical treatment for her son. The interview took place in the "Emek" hospital during one of these visits.

Interviewer: Hello Soha.

Soha: Hello.

Interviewer: OK, you know this is an interview we are doing for a project about the Israeli–Palestinian conflict, right?

Soha: Yes.

Interviewer: Good. So I will ask you about that in a minute, but first, tell me something about yourself.

Soha: My name is Soha, I am 36 years old, I live in (the West Bank city of) Jenin. I have seven children: four boys and three girls, and I hope to have more children in the near future. I was married when I was 16 years old with Ahmed, who works as a builder. My oldest daughter, Samara, is 19 years old. She has a son, he is one and a half years old. When she was born I was only 17. The next is Jamil, he is 18 and he is already engaged, he is before the wedding. The next is Muhamed, he is 16 he is a good student and he has good grades at school. The next is Rula, she is 13. She studies at junior high school. The next is Nazira, she is 11 and she has danced all her life and she studies at primary school. The next is Said, who is 5 and he is in the kindergarten. And finally, the last one is Hassan. He is only 3 years old, he is nice and naughty. He is a very good boy but he is unfortunate because he suffers a lot. About a year and a half ago we found that he has a problem with his kidneys and he needs a kidney transplant and now we are waiting for a charity to help us or for a miracle. For over a year and a half we have had treatments and checkups all the time. On one occasion we had to do dialysis for Hassan for three consecutive days because his kidneys don't work well. We need to clean them with this dialysis, it is a tool that cleans the kidneys, but after his treatment, he always feels very bad. This treatment is very hard for him, my boy is very sad and we are praying all the time to find a donor for him and to pass this trouble as fast as possible.

Interviewer: Do you do all the treatments in the hospital "Emek"? (The Emek hospital is an Israeli hospital located in Afula, a midsize city in northern Israel.)

Soha: Yes, it's a luck that it is near our home.

Interviewer: Thank you. OK, so regarding the Israeli–Palestinian conflict, can you tell me if you belong or identify yourself with any political group?

Soha: I identify myself with the Hamas movement. I support them and now I believe that we need to get all the lands returned. This land belonged to us and to our fathers, and you took it from us by force, therefore we will fight by force too until we will return to our lands and Jerusalem, the Holy Land that belongs to us. We will fight at any price and if we need to use terror by attacks and violence, I am ready for everything to return our honor, our independence, and the Palestine that was taken from us.

Interviewer: May I ask you what do you think about Israeli–Palestinian conflict?

Soha: Yes, please, I have nothing to hide, I think we have no solution for this problem, we tried to solve it many times and we didn't succeed. For example, the Oslo Agreement with Rabin and Arafat. I was sure then that it will bring peace and I even supported the peace in the Oslo Agreement. But not now. I have changed my mind, and a lot of our leaders changed too. Rabin was murdered and all the leaders after him didn't follow his way, they only want to destroy us.

Interviewer: Why do you think we cannot find a solution for the Israeli–Palestinian conflict?

Soha: Now we have a lot of hate between the sides and everything seems lost.

Interviewer: Did you have any experience that caused you to change your mind?

Soha: Yes, since the time I have been running from one hospital to another hospital, and I have had to meet Jews, and I have seen their behavior to me and my children, and I can see the hate and anger in their eyes, I understood that there is no chance for peace, and there will never be.

Our only alternative is to fight them and to return them to Europe or USA, but not in our land.

Interviewer: Can you tell about any situation that you experienced with the Jews?

Soha: Any time me and my family need to cross the border to arrive to the hospital, we have a lot of problems. We need many approvals and permits and we need to wait a lot of time at the border. We need to arrive several hours before to be able to cross the border because it is a very long line and most of the time they check everyone and their luggage and everybody has to go through a body check even if a person who has all the approvals to cross the border. I always get on my way with long before I have to arrive because I don't know how much time I will need to wait in the line, but I know that I still have to be in the hospital at a specific hour. About eight months ago my son had an attack and he didn't feel well and we took him quickly to the hospital, my husband and me. When we arrived to the border they began to make us problems, humiliate us, the soldiers beat my husband. They didn't believe us that we needed to arrive fast to the hospital. We didn't have approvals because Hassan didn't feel well suddenly and we didn't have a specific appointment hour in the hospital because it was a sudden attack. We thought we will lose him. The soldiers in the border are so cruel, they see a little boy who is sick and they have no compassion, they make problems and they don't take that into account, humiliate us, shout at us, curse us, push us. They didn't want to give us permission to enter. I screamed, I cried, I begged them to give us permission to arrive to the hospital. My son was dying and the soldiers didn't care about it. At the end, after a long time and after confirmation from the hospital they gave me and Hassan permission to enter but didn't give it to my husband, it is so cruel. After all these humiliation which happens almost everyday and all the hate I see in the soldiers and in the hospital, in the Jewish doctors and nurses, all the different behavior and discrimination because we are Arabs, and they give us disrespect while they don't do problems to Jewish patients and don't make them wait a long time for each treatment. When they see that I am from Palestine I can feel the hatred in the air and I can see in their eyes they are disgusted to touch us and to help us. Every time I need something from the nurses and doctors it takes a long time, but when a Jew asks for something, they immediately run to help him. We have no choice, we will continue to make terror attacks and to attack the Jews as much as possible, until they run from here and we'll return to live in Palestine as we want it. It's our land and the Jews have no rights here. The Jews understand only violence and the use of force.

Interviewer: From all you said, I understand that you are extreme in your mind. Don't you think we could have any chance to live together?

Soha: You tell me. How can I think there is any chance at all after this behavior, the hatred, the humiliation, the discrimination, and the lack of compassion? Unfortunately, I can't see any chance of this in my opinion.

HATE: THE PSYCHOLOGY OF EXTREMISM, DEHUMANIZATION, AND VIOLENCE

At least two thirds of our miseries spring from human stupidity, human malice and those great motivators and justifiers of malice and stupidity, idealism, dogmatism and proselytizing zeal on behalf of religious or political idols.

Aldous Leonard Huxley, British writer

We could easily argue that in 2004, it was Osama bin Laden, by masterminding the 9/11 terror attacks against the World Trade Center and the Pentagon, who actually led to the election of George W. Bush to the Presidency of the United States. Similarly, in February 1996, it was probably Islamic militants, who carried out a series of suicide bombings in Tel Aviv, who gave the elections in Israel, three months later, to the right-wing leader of the Likud party, Benjamin Netanyahu, instead of the moderate Nobel Prize winner and Labor party candidate Shimon Peres. And finally, it was without a doubt an Israeli extremist, Yigal Amir, who in 1995 assassinated then Israeli Prime Minister Yitzhak Rabin as he was coming out of a massive peace rally, who effectively brought to a screeching halt the then emerging peace process.

If it is true, on the one hand, that stereotypes, prejudice, and hatred are widespread phenomena among Israelis and Palestinians, therefore becoming a major barrier preventing peace, on the other, it is extremists, who, although much fewer in number, can carry the day because of their willingness to sacrifice life and plant terror. However, extremism doesn't exist in a vacuum. It is the result of a combination of sociocultural influences with individual characteristics that become the fertile ground for extremists to emerge.

What Makes an Extremist?

Is extremism something that is inherent, intrinsic to the individual, or is it something that is the result of external and social causes? Is it a combination of the two? A number of researchers have looked at the question of individual factors as the main influence in extremism, especially from the psychodynamic school of psychology, which is the contemporary successor to the original Sigmund Freud's psychoanalysis. For example, in one article, Hasanov[1] suggests that the concept of "inferiority complex," as proposed by the famous psychologist Alfred Adler, functions as a likely source of unconscious motivation to join radical, extremist, and fundamentalist movements. In his opinion, individuals who belong to stigmatized, discriminated, and/or prosecuted minority groups are more likely to suffer from an inferiority complex. As a consequence they "overcompensate" for the inferiority feelings by joining radical groups and committing extreme acts of violence, such as terrorism and suicide bombings. Another paper that explores the link between personality and extremism from a psychodynamic perspective was written by Schmidt, Joffé, and Davar.[2] They suggest that because of their autocratic nature, totalitarian regimes affect the process of identity formation in adolescence and the normal interaction between psychological mind structures (id, ego, and superego). This interference, for example, leads to a self-identity that is lacking in independence, and the state (or ideology) as a moral authority becomes the psychological basis for the extremism.

However, most research has failed to find a significant correlation between individual factors and extremism, and therefore contemporary theories of extremism and radicalism focus a lot less on psychopathological or personality explanations and a lot more on social and cognitive views. For these theories, extremism and radicalism are the result not of intrinsic factors but of a social context in which an external group, "the enemy," is highly hated, and at the same time the life circumstances of the in-group are harsh and even humiliating. In this case, the group will value and even admire extremists who are willing to sacrifice and fight for the cause and the welfare of the collective. Case in point, Palestinians who feel the daily effects of the humiliation of occupation value those willing to commit the ultimate sacrifice and become *shaheed,* a martyr who dies for the cause of fighting the enemy and restoring some measure of dignity to their people. Similarly, young Israeli settlers who move into remote areas of the occupied territories and are willing to withstand living in the middle of the "Arab enemy" to reclaim the land, which was wrongfully taken from the people of Israel, are seen as heroes and pioneers among their cultural group.

A significant number of studies support this social–cognitive approach to understanding extremism. For example, in a review of available research, Victoroff[3] argues that the data clearly show very little connection between psychological disorders and being part of a terrorist organization, and that the research tends to point to peer influence and increased social standing as major factors, together with negative experiences regarding the enemy group, such as incarceration or the death of a relative or a close friend.

Haslam and Turner,[4] in another review of available theories, also argue that personality variables, although somewhat related to radicalism and extremism, tend to have a weak relationship to them and that most of the research in this area is at best inconclusive. Instead, they explain that group membership, social identity, and social context are more important factors to determine political extremism than personality. They suggest that extremists look to enhance their own sense of self-identity, and by espousing extreme beliefs, consolidate their membership of and enhance their standing in the in-group.

Popular psychological writer Oliver James[5] also argues that, in the specific case of terrorism, there is little connection between personality and extremism. Instead, he focuses on research that suggests a combination of external factors. He suggests that it is mostly young people who have had humiliating experiences who are driven to join terrorist organizations when there is a social climate in which hatred of the out-group is an accepted norm and personal sacrifice is valued. In this case, extremism, and ultimately terrorism in general and suicide terrorism in particular, is the result of a combination of personal revenge together with social support and acceptance.

Psychologist John Ray also offers another interesting perspective to explain the emergence of radicalism.[6] He argues that political extremism is correlated to a very common phenomenon among Western youth: Sensation seeking. According to his theory, the same need for stimulation that drives an adolescent to attempt bungee jumping or paragliding would be connected with the excitement of joining these "underground" organizations that rebel against mainstream values.

Whatever the psychological causes of extremism, and in its ultimate form, terrorism, it is clear that by rejecting mainstream values, adopting a willingness for personal sacrifice, and having the ability to cause great amounts of pain and suffering to the out-group, the influence that extremist groups and individuals have on the continuation of the Israeli–Palestinian conflict is overwhelming. Both at the political and at the psychological levels, extremists in both camps have the ability to slow down and even stop any process of dialogue and reconciliation.

Extremism, Cultural Values, and Social Support

One of the main factors affecting the emergence of extremism and radicalism in any society is related to the sociocultural context of the particular country. In some cases, like Ireland or more recently Spain, radical organizations like the IRA (Irish Republican Army) and the Basque ETA (Euzkadi Ta Askatasuna) lay down their arms more as the result of a sociocultural change in which terrorism and violence became unacceptable among the general public than through the military efforts of the formal defense and security forces in the respective countries they were fighting, England and Spain. Conversely, a society in which bloodshed is seen as acceptable because of social circumstances or because of cultural values is much more likely to be fertile ground for radical violent organizations. Sadly, this is the case, to a degree, both among Israelis and among Palestinians. For example, according to an analysis by Dalsheim,[7] even among liberal Israelis, there is a "romantization" of representations of violence, in which the plight of the Palestinians is pretty much absent of the collective memory and the cultural narrative, and the acts of violence—even against civilians—associated with the Zionist enterprise are seen most of the time as justified and in some instances even as heroic. For instance, Dalsheim describes a history class in a *kibbutz,* a socialist cooperative farming community whose members tend to be on the progressive-liberal end of the political spectrum. The teacher is talking about the pioneer settlers of the period before the establishment of the State of Israel and is making great efforts to help the students connect personally with their plight. She describes them as heroes and mentions that "you have to admire these guys." The local Palestinians are totally absent from the narrative, and when a student asks a question about what is happening with them as the Jews start settling in the land (pushing the locals aside, as the student deducted), the teacher just dismisses the issue and avoids having to answer the question. On a different instance, Dalsheim describes a trip to the *Palmach* museum by a middle school classroom. The *Palmach* was the elite force of the *Haganah,* the pre-state defense army we referred to in the introduction to this book. She clearly shows how the museum romanticizes the war and at the same time completely ignores what is happening to the local Palestinian population, which as we discussed earlier, sees the exact same period in history as the great "disaster" in which they were uprooted from their homes and many of them fell victims of the violence.

This idealization of the war is a relatively mild example of how the social and cultural context among Jewish Israelis, even liberal ones, justifies and offers support to violence against Arabs and Palestinians. The situation, however, is much worse among the right-wing religious groups, and especially among settlers in the occupied territories. Bermanis and his colleagues[8] argue that in the past few years, a new right wing, extremist religious fundamentalist movement has emerged in Israel, which sees violence and even murder as justified by messianic values and believes that the Land of Israel rightly belongs to the Jewish people as a God-given right. These cultural beliefs support the emergence and justify the acts of extremists, such as Baruch Goldstein and Yigal Amir. Goldstein was a right wing, American-born Israeli who killed 29 Palestinians and injured more than 100 in 1994, in a shooting attack at the Cave of the Patriarchs in Hebron, a holy site revered both by Jews and by Muslims. Goldstein never faced justice for this racist crime since he was killed during his attack, and today there are several Web sites and memorials in Israel describing him as a "righteous man" and an heroic "avenger." The second case, Yigal Amir, on the other hand, is the convicted assassin of Israeli Prime Minister Yitzhak Rabin. Rabin was assassinated point-blank and in cold blood when he was leaving a peace rally in Tel Aviv. It was also the first time a high-level political figure was killed in modern Israel by another Jew, a fact that shocked and horrified most of the country. However, Amir is also the subject of numerous Web sites and articles calling him a "Hero," and there is a strong support movement among religious settlers calling for his release.

Among Palestinians, the situation is even more radical, since the support and justification of the use of violence is widespread. Not only is radical violence against Israelis regarded as justified, but being the victim

of Israeli violence is construed as a necessary right of passage into manhood, and those who die while attacking the Israelis receive the highest
honor of being named *shaheed,* literally a word that means "witness,"
but popularly construed among Muslims as meaning martyr and referring
to those Muslims who die during a *Jihad* or "holy struggle." According
to the sacred Muslim text, the *Hadith,* the *shaheed* will receive many
personal rewards, such as a place in paradise, forgiveness of his sins,
and the opportunity to intercede with Allah for his friends and relatives.
While it is important to mention that many Muslim scholars do not
see *Jihad* necessarily as a physical war and a violent struggle against the
enemies of Islam, it is also important to point out that most Palestinians
do see their conflict against Israel as a *Jihad,* and those who die fighting it
as *shaheeds.*

In one study, Peteet[9] argues that among Palestinian adolescents, confronting and being arrested by the Israeli military or police is interpreted
as a "rite of passage" into manhood. Young Palestinians are encouraged by
their peers and by some adults and become eager themselves to participate
in these rites. They might sometimes participate in stone throwing or
other confrontations precisely to construe their social sense of moral identity. Peteet argues that these perceptions of violence as a rite of passage
have become crucial among young Palestinians because it allows them
to perceive a reversal of the occupied–occupier relationship in which
Israel dominates and thus helps them create a strong sense of Palestinian
identity as tough and in control. This situation is exemplified in this
sample of one of the interviews we conducted. The interviewee is Chaled,
a young Palestinian man from the city of Tira, in the West Bank (Interviewer: Fedalia Maram):

Interviewer: Is there a specific rite to go from childhood to adulthood
(among the Palestinians)?

Chaled: Not generally, there is nothing specific but you reach the peak
of your manhood when you get mature understanding and way of thinking, and physical maturity. Then you get married and raise a family
and bring children and that's when you are considered to have reached
manhood. If you don't bring children then your manhood would be
lacking in the eyes of others.

Interviewer: What about displaying physical violence against the Israeli
army, could that be seen as a rite of passage?

Chaled: Of course. A youth that attempts to defend the house's women, children, and the elderly certainly will be considered in a different way, specially if he is successful in defending them, even if they arrest him.

Interviewer: If he is arrested, what will be the situation after he is released?

Chaled: The moment he comes back home the family and even the extended family will welcome him with greater respect and appreciation and will bless him upon his return and long term will regard him differently.

The social and cultural support radical violence enjoys among Israelis and Palestinians is, unfortunately, not relegated to fringe groups or to specific segments of the population. There is at least a baseline widespread tolerance toward violence from the in-group that allows the radical groups to thrive and that is reflected in self-serving perceptions of the generalized and protracted level of hostility. Therefore, people on both sides tend to justify the use of violence against the out-group, while at the same time inflating condemnation of the use of violence against the in-group. One example is a study by the joint Israeli–Palestinian research team of Shamir and Shikaki.[10] In their study, Shamir and Shikaki conducted surveys among more than 2,300 participants, Israeli Jews, Israeli Arabs, and Palestinians, asking them whether eleven different acts of violence, some local and some international, would be considered "terrorism." They were asked to state their personal opinion but also to say what they thought the "international community" would think about each incident. The incidents included a number of clearer instances, some of Palestinian attacks against Israelis, such as the Palestinian suicide bombing of the "Dolphinarium" club, a discotheque popular among teenagers, in which twenty-one Israeli civilians were killed, and some instances of Israeli attacks against civilian Palestinians, like the Baruch Goldstein incident we discussed above. It also included some more ambiguous ones like Palestinian shootings or Israeli military operations, and finally, some international ones: the 9/11 Twin Towers attack, the Pan Am jet bombing over Lockerbie, Scotland, and the anthrax scare where biowarfare spores were sent through the mail in the United States. The results from the Shamir and Shikaki study were astonishing. First, Israeli Jews and Palestinians present a strikingly self-serving "mirror image" of their opinion, in which violence by their in-group was pretty much justified, while violence by the out-group was largely perceived as terrorism. Second, both groups presented what Shamir and Shikaki call a "hostile world" perception, in which both groups believe the international community is biased against them and tends to be more negative toward their acts than toward the acts of their enemies. And finally, regarding the international incidents, while Israelis almost unanimously considered them to be terrorism, the Palestinians were more ambiguous about it. This last result, according to the authors, fits the self-serving bias pattern due to the fact that most of these incidents were perpetrated by Muslims.

Another example of this general level of justification can be observed in a study by Punamaki[11] (reported by Jagodic).[12] In this study, 185 Israeli and 128 Palestinian children aged 9 to 13 were given a questionnaire regarding their attitudes toward war and violence. They were asked questions in four areas: moral judgment of war in general (e.g., War is always a bad thing), justification of their own nation's fight (e.g., My people had no options but to fight), loyalty and the sense of duty in war (e.g., It is an honor to die for one's country), and attitudes to the possibility of peace (e.g., It is possible to stop outbreaks of war). Punamaki found some results which are consistent with the idea of a general sense of justification of violence. For example, 72% of Israeli and 81% of Palestinian children believe that war is sometimes necessary, while 80% and 86% respectively believe that war sometimes has good effects. However, there are some differences. For instance, 87% of the Palestinian children believe war is an exciting experience, while only 32% of Israeli children do. Similarly, while both Israeli and Palestinian children tended to justify their nation's own fighting, Palestinians are more inclined to do so. For example, 71% of Palestinian children support their nation's decision to fight compared to 52% of Israelis. Finally, both groups demonstrated a very high degree of loyalty and duty. For example, 87% of Israelis and 92% of Palestinians believe that it is a good thing to "die for your country."

In summary, it is quite clear that both societies and cultures have an overall sense of social support and underlying values that justify and even revere those in their in-group who are willing to fight and sacrifice themselves for their nation. This, as we mentioned before, is one of the conditions that facilitate the emergence of radical violent groups, but it is not the only one. In order for the society to become a more fertile ground for extremism, it is also important that the context, whether socioeconomical or political, encourages its emergence.

Contextual Factors in Israeli–Palestinian Extremism

As we have reviewed before, extremism and radicalism tend to emerge in societies where the external context is such that there is a general sense of despair and hopelessness, whether because of socio-economic conditions, because of the physical threat of violence, or because of political oppression.[13] It is important to note, however, that it is not the *individual* level of poverty or lack of education that drives extremists. As many journalists pointed out after the 9/11 attacks, the terrorists tended to be well educated and from the middle class. In other words, it is the *social* sense of despair that motivates people, many times well educated and financially stable, to become radicals. A number of studies support this view and have found that there is little correlation between individual level poverty or education and terrorism. For example, von Hippel[14] notes that many suicide bombers and terrorist leaders are actually better educated and better off economically than the average of their peers, and Krueger and Malečková,[15] in a survey of Arab terrorism, found little connection between socio-economic indicators and terrorist activity. They instead suggest that terrorism was probably better explained by political beliefs and feelings of indignity and frustration among the oppressed groups. Nevertheless, precisely because the contextual roots of extremism are more the result of a *psychological perception* of injustice and not of a real socioeconomic disadvantage, socioeconomic conditions do play a crucial role in the emergence of extremism. If these dreadful living conditions are perceived as a result of the oppression, then they are more likely to trigger the rage and hate that increase the tendency toward extremism, in particular among those who are slightly better educated and better off economically, who would be more likely to draw this assumption and become more active in what they perceive as a struggle for justice.

The Israeli and Palestinian cases are not the exception. In one study, for instance, Dabbagh[16] reviews the narrative of thirty-one Palestinians who attempted and failed to commit suicide, some of them by carrying out suicide bombings. Dabbagh links these attempts to a sense of social despair and helplessness, and she concludes that becoming a martyr is "one way in which these men who had neither employment nor families could gain social status, or social capital" (p. 216). In one example, one of her subjects explained:

Yes, I think of death. For example, I sit and think why God created us, the Palestinian people in particular. God created us and from the beginning we woke up in the world and we are under occupation. I mean, it's true we're living in the world...but it feels like a jail (p. 215).

In another example, Pedahzur and Canetti-Nisim[17] propose in one paper an integrative model to explain the rise of right-wing extremist ideology in Israel. They conducted a study in which they interviewed over 1,000 Israeli Jews from diverse backgrounds (settlers from the occupied territories, ultraorthodox Jews, residents of the largely poverty-stricken "development towns," new emigrants, etc.). They asked questions regarding support for right-wing extremist ideology, group identity, and socioeconomic and demographic variables. Pedahzur and Canetti-Nisim found a number of different significant correlations. For example, both education and income level were negatively correlated to right-wing extremism, supporting the idea that people who are poorly educated and economically disadvantaged have a higher tendency toward extremist ideologies. In their overall conclusions, Pedahzur and Canetti-Nisim explain that in order to better explain support for right-wing extremism, it is necessary to have a model that also includes "imagined economic or political threats, perceived competitive conditions, or other psychological mechanisms, which operate to reinforce the role of individual socioeconomic conditions" (p. 20). In other words, it is not necessarily the poverty and the hardships that lead to radicalism, but the perception and belief that these are caused by injustice and oppression. Pedahzur and Canetti-Nisim conclude that while poverty, deprivation, a sense of lack of security and control over your life are not necessarily the only or most direct factors that will lead to the emergence of radicalism, they certainly play a major role.

This last point is illustrated in a study by Israeli researcher Moore.[18] Moore sent questionnaires to over 5,000 Jewish and 1,300 Palestinian high school students and asked about their expectations for the future [e.g., "Ten years from today, how likely are you to (a) be married, (b) have your own home, (c) hold a steady job..." (p. 527)], their sense of personal deprivation [e.g., "When you compare yourself with others, is what you receive in life (a) much more than I expect; (b) more than I expect; (c) about what I expect; (d) less than I expect" (p. 528)], and their sense of control [e.g., "In your opinion how well does each characteristic fit you?; ambitious, analytical, competitive, decisive, leadership ability..." (p. 528)]. First, Moore found that there were significant differences between the Jewish students and the Palestinian students. For example, Palestinian students had a significantly stronger sense of personal deprivation and lower expectations of the future. Moreover, Moore also found that Palestinian students from socioeconomically disadvantaged strata had an even lower level of expectations for the future, suggesting a strong relationship between personal deprivation, a personal sense of pessimism, and ultimately, feeling no control over your life. Therefore, as we have previously discussed, it is fair to assume that the perception of the harsher economic, political, and social context that Palestinians have to endure as the result of Israeli discrimination will increase their tendency toward participation in extremist and radical organizations and support for their ideologies.

Similarly, Haddad[19] conducted a study in which he interviewed two populations: Palestinian refugees living in southern Lebanon and Lebanese Muslims. He found that support for suicide bombings among both populations was largely a function of low income, and for the Palestinians it was also correlated to residence in refugee camps, whose conditions are generally deplorable. These results once again reinforce the conclusion that perception of injustice and control over your life play a major role in the support of extremism. An interesting finding that we will review more extensively below is that support for suicide bombing was significantly higher among women than men.

This last point leads to another interesting illustration of how contextual factors can enhance the tendency toward increased radicalism from a study by Weinbaum.[20] In her study, Weinbaum reviews the oral history of Israeli and Palestinian women. Her main conclusion is that in some circumstances, and contrary to the common stereotype that mothers tend to be antiwar and pro-peace, having children is an event that actually is more likely to *radicalize* the activism of Israeli and Palestinian women. She argues that precisely because of the protective and nurturing character of the mothering role, mothers are more willing to sacrifice and to act to battle the enemy if they perceive that the situational context is a threat for the welfare of their children. In one example, Weinbaum interviews "Ronit," an Israeli feminist leader, who explains that "her propulsion into a national leadership role was precipitated in response to the perceived threat to the life of her son" (p. 26). In a similar fashion, we have numerous examples like that of Palestinian mother Naima al-Obeid, who appeared in a shocking interview on CNN in 2002, after her son, who joined a radical Palestinian organization with her full support, was killed in a gun battle with Israelis. In her interview, Naima not only was proud and supportive of her son's sacrifice but quickly asserted that in the name of the struggle to liberate Palestine, she had eight more children to sacrifice. She immediately received numerous calls of support from fellow Palestinians and Muslims all around the Arab world. Initially, Naima might have been pushed to a position in which the despair, the humiliation, and the insecurity of her situation made her adopt a very paradoxical, and even illogical, position vis-à-vis the welfare of her family. However, as the media attention that she received suggested, and the countless expressions of support and admiration that she received from Palestinians, as well as from Arabs and Muslims all around the world, for her willingness to sacrifice, showed there is one more personal element that we need to discuss if we want to better understand the psychology of extremism: In a society in which there is social support for dramatic acts of violent sacrifice, extremism can be construed as heroism.

Extremism, Suicide, and Heroism

In the movie *Paradise Now* by Palestinian director Hany Abu-Assad, two friends, Said and Khaled, are recruited by a radical organization to commit a suicide bombing in Israel. By all accounts, Said and Khaled are average young Palestinians, neither religious fanatics nor ideologically committed to the organization. In fact, they are not even active members but are recruited by the cell from the outside only to become martyrs, and specially selected because, for different reasons, they are personally vulnerable to the pressure. It is hard for them to say no, and once they accept, even harder to change their minds. First, because of the expected rewards, both in economic terms and in honor and prestige that they know will take place for their families. Second, because of the social and cultural pressure, the stigma and the shame it would bring them and their loved ones if they were to yield to their fears and to their consciences. It is also a superbly researched film that accurately represents the psychological and social processes that lead to the phenomenon of suicide bombings.

I wanted to explore the topic of suicide bombings in a separate section, because it is a unique phenomenon that has a specially powerful impact and has been thoroughly reviewed in recent years after the 9/11 World Trade Center attacks. There are plenty of contemporary writings regarding the topic in general and Palestinian suicide attacks in particular.

For instance, in her book *Dying to Kill: The Allure of Suicide Terror,*[21] Bloom explores a number of factors that lead to the use of suicide bombings. She highlights some important issues regarding suicide bombers; for example, it does not seem to be a phenomenon that is tied to intrinsic, individual causes. She explains that there have not been any successful attempts to profile suicide bombers since they not only vary across socio-economic status, age, and sex but seem to share little in terms of psychological profiles. On the other hand, there seem to be clear extrinsic, social, and group-related causes that explain the suicide bombing phenomenon. Bloom found common organizational and strategic factors that lead to suicide bombings as a rational strategy to attain both internal and external goals. For example, extremist groups will use the tactic to compete for internal social support, and at the same time, to attempt to demoralize an enemy who is perceived as more powerful. Bloom, however, does not devote too much of her study to try to understand the individual motivation a person might have to become a suicide bomber. Even if a radical organization makes a rational decision to use suicide as a strategic weapon, how do they convince the individual people, who we have already discussed come from a variety of social and personality backgrounds, to go ahead and commit the ultimate sacrifice? Battin,[22] for example, suggests that current psychological models that attempt to explain individual motivation to be a suicide bomber in terms of "suicide models" are inadequate since suicide bombers tend to understand their acts more as "martyrdom," a sacrifice for the good of the people, rather than suicide. Furthermore, Battin explains that models that look at the phenomenon in terms of mental illness or psychopathology do not contribute to the understanding of suicide bombing since the vast majority of volunteers do not fulfill a psychopathological profile. A number of observers, such as Dickey, Mark, and Scott,[23] Ganor,[24] and Rubin,[25] have suggested that most of these suicide bombers are young men with deep beliefs, usually religious, but sometimes just ideological. However, because a number of suicide bombers have been from secular organizations and the level of religious/ideological commitment varies, explanations that focus on religious beliefs are at best partial. On the other hand, Merari,[26] who has researched suicide bombing extensively, suggests that the willingness to volunteer to become a suicide bomber is not associated with individual characteristics nor religion nor poverty. Instead, he proposes that it is rather the outcome of manipulative group influences, in which the radical groups use a variety of "persuasive" and "group pressure" techniques to corner the prospect bomber to make a commitment, at which point they enter a social and psychological spiral from which it is extremely difficult to escape.

Pedahzur, Perliger, and Weinberg[27] have attempted to integrate these ideas by analyzing a profile database of 819 Palestinian terrorists, 80 of which were suicide bombers. They integrated their findings into a theory that proposes that individual willingness to volunteer for a suicide bombing is in fact a combination of two factors: on the one hand, the volunteer ultimately perceives himself or herself as a deeply committed member of the collective and by carrying out the suicide attack he or she is making a valued and rewarded sacrifice for the collective—termed "altruistic suicide"; on the other hand, the volunteer is driven by a sense of hopelessness, a situation of oppression from which there is no escape and the only dignified escape from a life that is perceived as meaningless is to commit suicide and at the same time revenge—or "fatalistic suicide." For the first factor, a deep process of social persuasion and group pressure is important to convince the volunteer that the sacrifice is worthy and highly valued by the collective. For the second factor, a perceived reality of oppression (like the Israeli occupation in the Palestinian case) and lack of freedom is necessary.

This view is also supported by a study performed by Moghadam.[28] He analyzed the patterns of Palestinian suicide bombings in the period of September 2000 to June 2002, and he concluded that suicide bombings are a phenomenon in which individual and organization factors have to be seen in an integrated manner. He proposes a two-phase process that leads to suicide bombings. On the first stage, the "motivation phase," a number of factors prime the prospective volunteer, usually a young male still in a stage of identity development and therefore more vulnerable to manipulation and ideological beliefs. Some of these factors would be what Pedahzur and his colleagues consider altruistic, like religious, nationalist, and sociological factors. Others, like personal, economic, and psychological factors, would be more closely associated with fatalistic factors. In Moghadam's analysis, in the first phase these factors interact to motivate the volunteer. In the second stage, the "institutional phase," radical organizations take advantage of these factors to recruit the volunteers (who are usually neither active members of the organizations, nor close friends or family of the organization's leadership) and to "train" them through a mixture of anti-Israeli propaganda and religious indoctrination. It is during this critical phase that the volunteer becomes thoroughly convinced that the suicide attack is the highest sacrifice for the welfare of the Palestinian people and that his martyrdom will bring great honor and rewards to him (posthumously, as a hero, and in the afterlife, where he will be duly rewarded), to his family, and to his people.

In summary, it is quite clear from the research that we cannot dismiss suicide bombings as a fringe issue and suicide volunteers as pathological types. It is a phenomenon that most certainly includes some factors that are shamelessly exploited by radical organizations, with others that are the result of the perception of hopelessness created by the dreadful conditions and the humiliation of the Israeli occupation.

Chapter Conclusion

Extremism is a vicious circle. On the one hand, it is fueled by social, cultural, and contextual factors that create a fertile ground in which extremism is not only not condemned but to a certain degree even celebrated. On the other hand, once the beast is born, it will do whatever it can to self-perpetuate. Extremism promotes the conflict, which is the original reason why it is tolerated and praised, and every time a solution is on the horizon that might lead to the end of the conflict, extremists on both sides of the conflict will do everything in their power to torpedo those initiatives. The power, the status, and the social respect that extremists enjoy during conflict will evaporate if a solution is found, and therefore it is clearly in their interest to try to continue the conflict. In the short-term, mainstream Israelis and Palestinians have supported and continue to tolerate and even support extremists because it seemed like they served their interest in the conflict. But in the long-term, this support has backfired. For example, according to Amon,[29] Israeli governments, after the 1967 war, began to support Zionist orthodox Jews who were willing to move into the occupied territories because of religious and messianic reasons, because their willingness was congruent with the strategic policies of the government. As a result, they provided them with massive infrastructure, economic incentives, and military support that both strengthened them and legitimized them in the eyes of the average Israeli. This policy backfired years later. Not only because it became a breeding ground for extremists willing to commit political assassination, but also because it generated a movement that would later prove very difficult to negotiate with when opportunities to promote peace became possible, like the 2005 Gaza Strip withdrawal. For the Palestinians too, the support that Yasser Arafat and the Palestinian leadership gave to the radical groups during the years of Intifada backfired when the new Palestinian president, Mahmud Abbas (Abu Mazen), tried to reach an agreement with Israel and ultimately his party lost the legislative elections to the more radical Hamas group.

In conclusion, extremism is a phenomenon that can only be dealt with by removing the factors that lead to the legitimization and social support of its tactics. Mainstream Israelis and Palestinians must also understand that reversing course and backtracking on peace initiatives every time extremist groups carry out attacks specifically designed to sabotage those initiatives only plays into the hands of extremists and harms the moderates. Only when the mainstream population is willing to stop tolerating and start condemning extremists, will extremism slowly begin to dissipate. However, this is a slow process that requires bold decisions by the leadership and patience by the people, both of which are in short supply among Israelis and Palestinians. In the meantime, there will be extremism, there will be violence. And there will be pain.

Notes

1. Eldar Hasanov, "Religious and National Radicalism in Middle-Eastern Countries: A Psychoanalytical Point of View," *International Forum of Psychoanalysis* 14, no. 2 (2005): 120–22.

2. Catherine Schmidt, George Joffé, and Elisha Davar, "The Psychology of Political Extremism," *Cambridge Review of International Affairs* 18, no. 1 (2005): 151–72.

3. Jeff Victoroff, "The Mind of the Terrorist: A Review and Critique of Psychological Approaches," *Journal of Conflict Resolution* 49, no. 1 (2005): 3–42.

4. S. Alexander Haslam and John C. Turner, "Extremism and Deviance: Beyond Taxonomy and Bias," *Social Research* 65, no. 2 (1998): 435–48.

5. Oliver James, "What Turns a Man into a Terrorist?" *New Statesman* 130, no. 4568 (2001): 36.

6. John J. Ray, "Political Radicals as Sensation-Seekers," *Journal of Social Psychology* 122, no. 2 (1984): 293.

7. Joyce Dalsheim, "Special Focus on Racism in Israeli Society," in "Settler Nationalism, Collective Memories of Violence and the 'Uncanny Other,'" *Social Identities: Journal for the Study of Race, Nation and Culture* 10, no. 2 (2004): 151–70.

8. Shai Bermanis, Daphna Canetti-Nisim, and Ami Pedahzur, "Religious Fundamentalism and the Extreme Right-Wing Camp in Israel," *Patterns of Prejudice* 38, no. 2 (2004): 159–76.

9. Julie Peteet, "Male Gender and Rituals of Resistance in the Palestinian Intifada: A Cultural Politics of Violence," *American Ethnologist* 21, no. 1 (1994): 31–49.

10. Jacob Shamir and Khalil Shikaki, "Self-Serving Perceptions of Terrorism Among Israelis and Palestinians," *Political Psychology* 23, no. 3 (2002): 537–57.

11. R.-L. Punamaki, *Childhood Under Conflict: The Attitudes and Emotional Life of Israeli and Palestinian Children* (Tampere: Tampere Peace Research Institute, Research Reports, 1987).

12. Gordana Kuterovac Jagodic, "Is War a Good or a Bad Thing? The Attitudes of Croatian, Israeli, and Palestinian Children Toward War," *International Journal of Psychology* 35, no. 6 (2000): 241–57.

13. See, for example, M. Lubbers and P. Scheepers, "Individual and Contextual Characteristics of the German Extreme Right-Wing Vote in the 1990s: A Test of Complementary Theories," *European Journal of Political Research* 38, no. 1 (2000): 63–94; M. Lubbers and P. Scheepers, "Explaining the Trend in Extreme Right-Wing Voting: Germany 1989–1998," *European Sociological Review* 17 (2001): 431–49; M. Lubbers and P. Scheepers, "French Front National Voting: A Micro and Macro Perspective," *Ethnic and Racial Studies* 25 (2002): 120–49; M. Lubbers, P. Scheepers, and J. Billiet, "Multilevel Modeling of Vlaams Blok Voting: Individual and Contextual Characteristics of the Vlaams Blok Vote," *Acta Politica* 35 (2000): 363–98; M. Lubbers, M. Gijsberts, and P. Scheepers, "Extreme Right-Wing Voting in Western Europe," *European Journal of Political Research* 41 (2002): 345–78.

14. K. von Hippel, "The Roots of Terrorism: Probing the Myths," *Political Quarterly* 73, Suppl. 1 (2002): 25–39.

15. Alan B. Krueger and Jitka Malecková, "Education, Poverty, and Terrorism: Is There a Causal Connection?" *Journal of Economic Perspectives* (Fall 2003): 119–44.

16. Nadia Taysir Dabbagh, "Narrative Expressions of Despair Under Occupation," *Anthropology & Medicine* 11, no. 2 (2004): 201–20.

17. Ami Pedahzur and Daphna Canetti-Nisim, "Support for Right-Wing Extremist Ideology: Socio-Economic Indicators and Socio-Psychological Mechanisms of Social Identification," *Comparative Sociology* 3, no. 1 (2004): 1–36.

18. Dahlia Moore, "Perceptions of Sense of Control, Relative Deprivation, and Expectations of Young Jews and Palestinians in Israel," *Journal of Social Psychology* 143, no. 4 (2003): 521–40.

19. Simon Haddad, "A Comparative Study of Lebanese and Palestinian Perceptions of Suicide Bombings: The Role of Militant Islam and Socio-Economic Status," *International Journal of Comparative Sociology* 45, no. 5 (2004): 337–63.

20. Batya Weinbaum, "The Radicalizing Impact of Children on Mother's Activism: Insight From Oral Histories With Some Jewish Israeli Mothers, Summer 1999," *Journal of Feminist Family Therapy* 13, no. 4 (2001): 23–40.

21. Mia Bloom, *Dying to Kill: The Allure of Suicide Terror* (New York, NY: Columbia University Press, 2005).

22. Margaret P. Battin, "The Ethics of Self-Sacrifice: What's Wrong with Suicide Bombing?" *Archives of Suicide Research* 8, no. 1 (2004): 29–36.

23. Christopher Dickey, Mark Hosenball, and Scott Johnson, "Training for Terror," *Newsweek*, 2001, 42.

24. Bohaz Ganor, "Suicide Terrorism: An Overview," in *Countering Suicide Terrorism* (Herzlia: ICT, 2000), 134–45.

25. Elizabeth Rubin, "The Most Wanted Palestinian," *New York Times Magazine,* June 30, 2002, 26–31, 42, 51–55.

26. Ariel Merari, "Suicide Terrorism," in *Assessment, Treatment, and Prevention of Suicidal Behavior,* ed. Robert I. Yufit and David Lester (Hoboken, NJ: John Wiley & Sons, Inc., 2005), 431–53; Ariel Merari, "The Readiness to Kill and Die," in *Origins of Terrorism,* ed. William Reich (Cambridge, MA: Cambridge University Press, 1990), 192–207.

27. Ami Pedahzur, Arie Perliger, and Leonard Weinberg, "Altruism and Fatalism: The Characteristics of Palestinian Suicide Terrorists," *Deviant Behavior* 24, no. 4 (2003): 405–23.

28. Assaf Moghadam, "Palestinian Suicide Terrorism in the Second Intifada: Motivations and Organizational Aspects," *Studies in Conflict and Terrorism* 26, no. 2 (2003): 65–92.

29. Moshe Amon, "Can Israel Survive the West Bank Settlements?" *Terrorism and Political Violence* 16, no. 1 (2004): 48–65.

INTERVIEWS

An Interview with Itamar, Who Lives in Bat-Ayin. Interviewer: Itzik Batito

Itamar, who lives in a Jewish settlement in the West Bank, is an active member of the extreme right wing in Israel.

Interviewer: Let's begin by you telling me about yourself.

Itamar: First of all, I'll present to you my personal identity. I'm Itamar, born in 1980. I'm 26 years old, and as you see, I am a resident of Bat-Ayin, which is considered a legal settlement. I am freshly married, about ten months, to my dear wife Malka. I was born in Israel and my parents were also born in the Israeli . . . the Holy Land, let it be built Amen. Well, let's continue. I am a son to my dear parents, and in addition I am the son of the King of Kings, the Holy One Blessed Be He, a father in heaven. I make a living, I maintain a small farm, in which I grow goats, and from them I do milk and cheese, and you know, thank God, I make a good living. This is it. What else will I tell you about myself. Oh, I remember, I am a relative of Noam Federman, well Noam Federman,* whom the police and the Shabac† don't leave for a moment. Now, look, in addition to all I have told you until now, which is some background about myself, I will add to you more details about myself. You'll see, as I have told you before we started the interview, I have no problem at all speaking with you and you recording it. But I'll tell you, I'm a man who defines himself as the extreme right, and I'll explain you what do I mean when I say it. My intention is that I don't believe in all these stupid agreements that our army and state try to do with the Arabs. I'll tell you this, there is no trust in Arabs even after forty years in grave. I'll even be more candid with you and tell you explicitly and unequivocally that I don't think that the Arab people has a right to exist at all, let alone exist and live in the State of Israel, and even more, they don't deserve a piece of land of the Holy Land, because as I was brought up and learned according to the Holy Torah, this state belongs to the people of Israel, and it is written in our sources. We Jews will receive the Land of Israel, and much more, the entire Land of Israel, that is, the Land of Israel with all its different parts, as it is stated in the Holy Torah. I'll tell you some other thing, look, don't

---

*Noam Federman, who lives in the West Bank city of Hebron, is a leader of the extreme right-wing Kach party. The Kach party was founded by extremist Rabbi Meir Kahane.
†The Shabac is abbreviation for Sherut Bitachon Clali or General Security Service. It is the internal security police force, parallel to the American FBI.

listen to those who talk about the '67 borders, and pardon me for the expression, all the shit they tell us and we give them territories unfortunately. I was not born in '67, and certainly not in '48, but from what I can tell you, the state...this land was promised to Abraham our ancestor, and he was our, and not the gentiles', father. Look, I was arrested many times by the police and the Shabac, and I'll tell you something. I have always been released one or two days afterward, because they did not have enough proof against me. I, personally, don't belong to the Kach (Kahane Chai) movement or other extremist movements, but what will I tell you, I support them, not economically (giggling), but I believe in their cause and their activity. Listen, they make a sacred work that our fearful state doesn't dare to do. They come up like men and do. These people know a lot of things, and they have a lot of experience, and therefore I rely on them more than on the Prime Minister or the Chief of Staff.

Interviewer: I see that you support a right-wing opinion, as you said before, that is, you are a right-wing activist. Can you tell me a little about this?

Itamar: Well, I'll start with the fact that I'm a right-wing activist, and I have been doing a lot during my life in the movement...Or rather, not exactly in the movement, but I have been active. It doesn't matter, but I support and agree with the activity of the right-wing movement, and even the extreme right, because they do a sacred work, and I'll explain to you what it means. They, as a group that cares about the country and they know what is real Zionism, try to prevent and reduce damages that would hurt people of the country and civilians, what the state tries to do, actually they do the opposite of what the state does, and most of the activists, who act in the extreme movements don't believe in the state law, neither in the authorities which impose the law in the country, like the police, the Shabac, and the court. Now look, we as the inhabitants of Bat-Ayin, I can tell you in the most obvious and unequivocal way that most of the inhabitants here are considered as right wing in their opinions, and at least half of the people are real activists, but I'll not go into it now. I wanted to tell you that we are one of the only settlement of all Israel which is not surrounded by a fence, and with God's help there will be no fence, and I, as long as I live, will see to it that there will be no fence. Why, I'll tell you why: if there is a fence it means that (a) you are afraid, and had you not been afraid, there wouldn't have been a fence, right? Now (b) the very fact that you put a fence, you divide into two parts. I mean this is mine and that is yours, and it isn't like that. Everything is ours, they have no ownership on any piece of land, do you see what I'm talking about? I think that our country is a country, which holds secular opinions. Look around, the country and the government are secular people, who have no idea about the Jewish religion they belong to, God will have mercy on them. And therefore, the movements of the extreme right and the people who are active there are shown in television as if they were beasts, but they are not like their descriptions. I'll give you an example. Take, for example, the detachment program (in Gaza). Look what happened. The Prime Minister and other members of the government gave the Palestinians the territories, over which they had fought twenty years ago, and until today they have been fighting for them. A lot of blood was shed on these lands, and they come and give it away, as if it were peanuts. Take Sharon, our Prime Minister. He is a hypocrite and corrupted, I'll tell you why. Because he is a big thief and a big corrupt, and for this he made the detachment program, so that he won't be judged for his lies. So, actually, he shifted the whole public debate, that is, instead of speaking about him in the news, about what he has done, and what he has taken, the news would be about the detachment. Had he been a real man, he wouldn't have done this move, and I know what I'm saying, because he used to say in former years that he was not ready to any steps that involved giving up parts of the country, and at last he did it himself. You have to know that I voted for him in the elections 4 years ago. If I had known that this was what he would do, over my dead body I would have voted for him. I would like to add another important thing in this matter of the detachment. Look, Sharon, the Prime Minister, is a person of weak character and a coward. That is, he is afraid of the US, and it is transparent, one can see it. If they push him a little, he gives in like a little child who has no personality, and who can't have a steady mind, and he has others to make decisions for him what to do. Now I'll return with you to the detachment program, and why do I support the position I support. Look, take all these, I mean the people who actually participated in the different activities for preventing the detachment program, (a) these are people who don't care about the country they live in and (b) the issue of uprooting of the settlements doesn't bother and irritate them. I, as a person, may think what I want, and I think that the Arabs have no right to exist at all, and I hold the opinion that all those who really belong, hold the same opinion, that is, see themselves as extremists. The extreme right in Israel is the target of the Shabac, and

I'll tell you quite clearly, I think that in order to achieve what we want, meaning to have quiet and good situation in our country, which belongs to us, we have to do everything so it will indeed be so. I mean any step we have to do, no matter what. Now, the State of Israel doesn't do everything it can to bring quiet and peace. Excuse me, what kind of peace? What are you talking about, with the Arabs there will never be peace, and whoever wants peace, we don't, we want to live here, and it doesn't matter what is the matter with them. And therefore the movements which are established by private people, who are defined as the extreme right, try indeed to bring about what we want, which is quiet in a country that belongs to us, with no Arabs, I repeat, with no Arabs. So, the people from the right, who really care about the State of Israel, and no one else. Don't listen to the stories they tell you on the news, nor in any other place.

Interviewer: Why do you support this opinion? Why do you support this position?

Itamar: Once again, I'll tell you that I support the opinion which says, as you know, we are Jews, and this is a Jewish state, and the Jewish state belongs to the Jews only, and therefore it is called the Jewish state. We made a mistake, not exactly we, but those who ran the country in 1948, and those who were in power at the time of the Independence War, and I'll tell you why, because they left the Arabs in the country, and what happens, many Arabs were left and the state has to provide them with a citizenship. The mistake was that they were not expelled then, all of them. Anyway, there was a war, and the Arabs were expelled, so why did you leave the "leftovers" of those who live with us today. It was a mistake, and I think that we pay for it today. You can see that everyday they do something else, that is, the Arabs who live here hurt the country and the security of the country everyday in another way, and there are many cases. In fact, each one of the Israeli Arabs who has an opportunity will bring terrorists here, and there are some who plan terrorist attacks both in the country and outside of it. Now these right-wing people really know what is the reality. Since most of them live near the Arabs in the different settlements, and they act according to the Sacred Torah in order to get rid of the Arabs. I hold my views because I see myself as the son of Father in Heaven, the Holy One Blessed Be He, and in his Sacred Torah he had given us this land. And he said to Abraham our ancestor that "To you I will give the Land of Canaan, your own land when you were a small people…" You see, the security of the country and its inhabitants is an outcome of the fortification of the family and education. If you have not been taught what it is the Land of Israel, if you are not loyal to your country, you transmit an unequivocal message to your enemies: come and take it from me! Thus, and thus only our security was lost for us. All the attempts of Oslo and the Road Map, which base our existence on accepting the justification of the enemy's claims, brought about more and more terror and death. In order to bring about quiet and security, there is a need of a totally opposite of this destructive trend. We have to return from the path of Oslo and impose Jewish sovereignty all over the territory of the Land of Israel that is in our hands, and I mean to conquer more territories, and not give them anything, you see what I say? I think that our state needs people who are…that means, who hold views like those who are called the extreme right, because those are the one who really do the job, believe me, and no one else.

Interviewer: Let me ask you about your opinion about Palestinians and Israelis, what do you think?

Itamar: First of all, Israelis, us, are the "chosen people." Now, as I have above mentioned, only us, the Israelis, the Jews, that is, have the right of existence in the State of Israel, and I would try to change the word Israelis to Jews. I'll tell you why Israelis. Because unfortunately there are people in Israel who are Israelis, but they are not Jews, and there is a problem. Now, look. I think that if we have already Arabs, and it doesn't matter what kind of Arabs, Israelis, or Palestinians, they have to serve us, as it is stated in the Sacred Torah: "People will work for you, nations will bow for you." And I tell you, there is no problem whatsoever, if all we hear that the settlers do to the Arabs, you know that they work for Jews, and they exploit them. I'll give you an example, and one can hear it a lot lately on television, that many settlers destroy olive trees that belong to Arabs, meaning Palestinians. Because I have told you several times, it is our country and there is no denying it. I'll tell you, listen, since the beginning of the Al-Aqsa Intifada there has been an increase in the number of terrorist attacks, which different Palestinian organizations execute against Israeli civilians. As a result of these severe attacks, hundreds of Israelis were killed and thousands were wounded, including many minors. Now look. The Palestinians are a shitty people, excuse me for the language, but they all deserve to be thrown into the sea, I tell you.

Interviewer: What do you think will be eventually the solution?

Itamar: There is no solution. There is no solution, and whoever tells you there is a solution, just says it in order to fish you. There is no solution, there is no end or a solution, I tell you this as you see, Arafat also was and has gone. We have brought Arafat from Tunisia. He promised us peace, and he brought us wars and the Intifada. It is Arafat I'm talking about. We have brought him from Tunisia, he was in Tunisia. You know, they didn't let him in. Then later they said, come on, we will give him the territories and he will make quiet for us and everything. . . We owned the Palestinian people from 1948, and at last he didn't give in of anything, and just made us an Intifada and troubles. Arafat was gone, and we have brought Abu Mazen. Abu Mazen wants to give up now, he wants to resign, he wants to escape, it is all stories, nothing has changed. We need a strong army, this is what I think to fight. We need a stronger army that what we have today and fight. Listen, how much the army can do these focused targets and all these nonsense? Twenty-four hours and only then the Palestinians will come and slaughter you in your home. I tell you the truth. They'll come, take you out of your house and kill you. They are fanatics, these Arabs, and I'm not an extremist, I just tell you what there really is. I'll give you the picture. The Palestinians, if they could come, they'll come to your house and take you out and cut off your head. . .the Palestinians. . .and they are also those who are in the Arab countries, those in Lebanon and in Iraq are all the same. They would lynch you, lynch you worse than the Nazis did to us. Listen well to what I'm telling you, worse than what the Nazis did to us, when they put us in these furnaces, they will put us. . .hanging. I'm not an extremist, I love them (laughter) I tell you the truth. I know already the whole history of this country, although I'm young, as you know. Young, I'm 26 years old, as I above-mentioned. All the time they said: everything would be alright, and they say it will be OK, it will be OK, and every time it becomes worse. They always say that next year would be better, we will bring peace, and such things. Always there will be peace, there will be peace. I tell you, the country doesn't want to make peace. In fact, it is not that they don't want to make peace, there is no one to make peace with. They don't want (the Palestinians). They don't want. They want the country, not the peace. It is finished. We gave them the territories, they don't want the territories, they don't want the territories, you have to understand that they want the country, not the territories. If we give them the territories there will be no peace, and you see it now. We have given them everything in Gaza Strip. You see what kind of peace it is, may their names be blotted out! now they want Tel Aviv and Haifa. Like it was in 1948, they want to throw us into the sea. I heard they talked about it in the beginning, before the territories. You don't know and you don't remember, but I heard from my parents and from their friends. And the hymn of the Palestinians was to throw us into the sea. And there was also their mentality...to fight. Let's leave the territories alone, let's put the territories aside. Let's start from 1967. They talked to us all the time...It was they who started wars, we didn't start wars. How did we take the territories, it was through a war that they started against us in 1967. After 1948 we were quiet, we didn't do any mess..., they started a war, and why? For what end? To throw us into the sea. Let's start from...1967, all right? So they started the Six-Day War, and then we conquered territories, and now we have all the troubles. We have given them back like suckers and idiots, pardon, and now they want the borders of 1948. We are dumb, talking only about the territories. They don't want the territories, they want us in the sea, they want the whole country. I don't make a difference between an Israeli Arab and an Arab from the territories; it is the same for me. An Israeli Arab and an Arab from the territories is the same, for me they are hand in hand. At the time of the Intifada, when these beasts from "Falestene," who made us the Intifada, the Arabs in Israel made us another Intifada here, inside. They are exactly like them. They are with them, you see, all the attacks in the country they have brought them upon us, they have brought the Palestinians here, they have brought them to do these attacks, they drove them with their cars 80%, but the state doesn't want to make a great noise out of this so that there would be no troubles. They, 80%, the attack in Haifa in the restaurant, this is an Arab from Um El-Fahem, and the Arab in Hadera, now, that is, the last attack that was now in Hadera, it was an Arab from Jat. I know everything, I don't sleep, believe me. All the attacks, 80%, are connected to Israeli Arabs. These two physicians who were caught as spies in Rumania, they got three years in jail with a break-fast and hotel conditions. They made a deal with them. These spies should have been thrown out in another country. In America people don't get less than forty years in jail, you see, you see the reality, you don't. They are all in tune with one another.

Interviewer: In your words above, you mentioned a number of times that there is no solution, and then you talked about different kinds of solutions, like using greater military force and others. Can you explain to me what was your intention?

Itamar: Look, I get sick of the Palestinians from day to another. I can't hear about them, and certainly not see them, I can't stand them. I think that we, Israelis, are stupid in one thing, which is that they don't erase them, and if you ask me, one has to do a holocaust to them, no peace. Not peace, holocaust, exterminate them from young to old, small in the belly, before he is born, after he is born. Erase them, I say. The solution I would think is the most appropriate, although I think there is no solution, is to cut them out, and every mistake there is, a missile. You see, not a house, to erase neighborhoods, to erase streets, and not to play games, and erase houses. I'll tell you, they are no suckers, these scoundrels, so you broke down their house, to the terrorists, I mean, so what, those he had killed in the terrorist attack will come back? It is not obvious that you do understand. Whoever wants to commit suicide, wouldn't do it because they are going to break down his house, (a) he won't need the house any more and (b) his family will build another house. You know, the Arabs are good builders. They have built us more than half of the country, if not all of it. They were born for building (laughter), a house is no problem to build, but a person is impossible to return. I think there will never be peace, and for peace there is a need of a strong war, to wipe their faces well, and that's it, let's see them, and also for the sake of frightening them. And for each mistake to wipe out a whole village or two, for each shooting on their part, even a shooting toward a driving car, and even if there were no people injured, to send a missile. I promise that in this way it will be possible to solve the story with them, and there will be no messing with them. And even with a machine gun. They won't use it, and surely will not attack. They will stop throwing stones and will not use weapons any more. They are a coward nation, they are a coward nation. All they do is out of fear, believe me. A person who goes out with a belt to commit suicide, it comes out of fear, and I'll tell you one more thing. It is true that when he explodes he takes with him more people, maybe tens of people, but their strength, their power they have accumulated until now is out of fear. Now look, the wise thing is to do something and get out of it alive, and I'll explain to you what does it mean. If you tell me that they come here, put the explosives and run away. So I'll answer you that this is bravery. You see, it is preferable to be alive in jail rather than die. Believe me, I have one person that

I know, and he is a Palestinian. I happened accidentally to talk to him, although I hate them to death, and he himself told me that it was just nonsense, and there is no such thing as seventy-two virgins. But who knows. No one has ever returned from there to tell us how it was there. You see.

Interviewer: Is there something more you would like to add?

Itamar: I'll tell you to sum up what I say. First of all the struggle against the detachment is a struggle about the survival of the State of Israel and about its image as a Jewish, democratic, and moral state. No arbitrary command that comes out of Sharon's office doesn't bind the public. Therefore, every citizen in the county must refuse to such a command with all his might. And I'll say it again that I am in favor of refuse, refuse, refuse. Yes, refuse a command, and I think that this is a right and brave deed. I have one more important thing to say about the Israelis and the Palestinians. Israelis against Palestinians, this is the way the State of Israel presents the picture. But, part of the Israelis are Arabs who help the bus exploders, and they are not loyal to the State of Israel. This is it, what else can I tell you. But I believe that God will help and we, his children, will do all we can, and everything will be all right. And I say that we will break down the Palestinians in all kinds of ways, like my brothers the settlers do in different places in the country, and this is the way to reach a state of rest and security, and it will be all right, you see? I don't believe in peace with Arabs, they are not people you can talk to, and I know what I'm telling you. I'll give you a last example before we finish. There were many Jews who employed Palestinians and helped them to make a living, and eventually, these beasts slaughtered them or murdered them, so there is no belief in none of the Arabs. They are not human beings you can talk to, and certainly not trust them. Another last example. You see what happened. Unfortunately they got the territories, God has mercy on those who gave, and with God's help he will not get away with it, and even pay him for doing this. And here you see them executing attacks and not stopping, let their names be blotted out.

An Interview with Hussein, Who Lives in Nazareth. Interviewers: Rim Laham, Rimah Isbanioli, and Lora Ramadan

Hussein is a 30-year-old professional, who used to live in the occupied territories but now lives inside Israel. He is married and has a young daughter. He used to be a member of the radical Peoples' Front for the Liberation of Palestine, and to this day, he supports their positions.

Interviewer: Tell me a little bit about yourself.

Hussein: My name is Hussein, I was born in Al Quds (Jerusalem) in the year 1976. I was a son in a family of ten people, including four brothers and four sisters. I finished my academic education in the State of Iraq, at Baghdad University, which took me about four years to complete. Today I am married, and have a 2-year-old daughter who we named "Philistin" (Palestine). Today I live in Nazareth and work as a manager in an international company.

Interviewer: I understand that you support a radical position, can you tell me a little bit about that topic?

Hussein: About twelve years ago I became a member in an organization called the "Popular Front for the Liberation of Palestine." It is an organization that calls to end the Palestinian–Israeli conflict in an "comprehensive" way. That means the liberation of the complete land of Palestine from the Jordan River to the Mediterranean Sea. To this day, I support any organization that calls for the destruction of the State of Israel. Because this is Palestinian land and it will remain Palestinian. The Jews came as parasites and controlled all the land, just so the Americans and the British could get rid of them, and therefore they supplied them with the Palestinian land in order for them to create their own country, which they call the Land of Israel in order to fulfill their Zionist dream.

Interviewer: Please allow me to ask you your opinion regarding Palestinians and Israelis. What do you think?

Hussein: As a Palestinian person I differentiate between the Arab and the Jew. If you have ever met a Jewish person in some country somewhere in the world, you relate to him like any other person who has his freedom and his rights. However, for me, I look at him like any other Jew who lives in the State of Israel, a parasite, a captor of the Palestinian territories, and whoever conquers my land, I will not greet him with roses, on the contrary, I will meet him with force that will lead ultimately to the end of the road, to the liberation of our land, the Land of Palestine. I see the Palestinian actions, the attacks inside the State of Israel, as heroic actions resulting from a natural reaction of any person subjected to repression, torture, and humiliation. And every person who sees his brother or some other relative, or a friend, who got killed in front of his eyes by the Israeli army, then you should expect from him that he will go ahead and blow himself up in the middle of Israel. We, as Palestinians, believe in the Palestinian Authority (the governing body in the Palestinian occupied territories), and we can see that every Jew who lives in the Palestinian territories automatically renounces all his civil rights and he is part of the Israeli occupation and supports the Israeli army. Every Jew in Israel has a number in the Israeli army, which means that at some point he will get a gun and go to the Palestinian areas to kill. I am sure that just like every person has different specific traits, like being good hearted, not to lie, etc., I am sure that all the Jews are murderers. Just because they conquered my land I hate every Jew.

Interviewer: Why did you join the Popular Front? Can you explain why do you support that position?

Hussein: I'll tell you a personal story that led me to support the organization and to my political opinions: At the end of the Intifada of the year 1988, there was a demonstration in the same neighborhood in which I live. Neither myself nor my brothers participated actively in this demonstration. However, at the same time, my brother got very very sick so we had to leave, me and him, to my uncle's house, who is a doctor and lives in the second floor. Suddenly, we saw the Israeli army inside the house and they arrested us (me and my brother) in spite of the fact that you could clearly see in my brothers face that he was ill. I was 12 years old back then. In any event, the Israeli army arrested both of us, and took us to the area where the demonstration was going on. There were lots of Israeli soldiers in that area. They beat us quite hard and asked us to confess that my brother was one of the organizers of the demonstration. Of course, I refused (because he did not organize it, but even if he had, I would not have told on him), so they said, "Well, then, look at this and think about it real well." They took my brother and they forced him to extinguish a fire that the demonstrators had started. That incident will never be erased from my memory and my thoughts, and nothing in the world will erase it. It will stay engraved in my memory.

Interviewer: What do you think will be the ultimate solution to the conflict?

Hussein: Solution? I don't think there is a solution because there is no middle point between good and evil. The Palestinian lands are our right, and the Israelis have to return to where they came from. And what is called "peace" it's a lie that the world has supported to promote the Israeli interests at the expense of the Palestinians. As I said before, I was a member in the Popular Front because it believes that the Israeli–Palestinian conflict is an existential conflict and not a conflict about money that you can divide between the two parties. Nobody has the right to give up our land and the blood of the martyrs, what Israel planted is death and violence and therefore that is the only thing it will get back from us. What the Israeli leaders call "the State of Israel" is a state for the Jews only, that means that they are racists and psychopaths, and therefore there is no way you can trust them or believe any of the Jews. In addition, I want to remind you I have lost one relative and seven friends who were killed by cold hands. Also, many lives have been decimated as a result of the strikes and the shots of the Israeli army, and therefore there is a source to my rage and my hate. The state of the Palestinian today is a state of death, arrests and house demolitions, of families emigrating. That is the situation of the Palestinian people, a situation that was caused by the Israeli occupation.

PAIN: TRAUMA AND THE PSYCHOLOGICAL CONSEQUENCES OF CONFLICT

Just as the body goes into shock after a physical trauma, so does the human psyche go into shock after the impact of a major loss.

Anne MacVicar Grant, Scottish Novelist

Ron, a young Israeli man who works as a yoga teacher, had a free afternoon and decided to meet an old friend to relax and have a coffee in a busy entertainment district in Tel Aviv. They were expecting to have a nice and quiet afternoon, but instead, they had the misfortune of selecting a coffee shop just across the street from a restaurant which, that day, became the target of a Palestinian suicide bomber. Several people died in the restaurant, but he was only moderately hurt as the result of the shrapnel and debris that flew all the way into the coffee shop. However, his physical scars were the least significant ones. The nightmares, the anxiety, the memories, all changed his life to a point where he could barely function, and left a lasting impression that will affect his life forever.

Maryam and Kamel, a married middle-aged Palestinian couple from Gaza, were harvesting a plot in their farm, and as is their custom, they were being helped by number of their children and grandchildren. Suddenly, a group of militants fired a mortar shell toward Israel from a nearby field about 100 yards away. The Israeli army retaliated by shelling the general area where the firing had occurred, and in the process, killed seven of the children, aged 11 to 16, who were working the patch. Maryam and Kamel lost four sons, a grandson, and a nephew. For them, and the remaining family who were also witnesses to the tragedy, the event changed their lives forever. Even several months later, when their son Mohammad, who had been in the hospital fighting for his life, finally died, Maryam reported that she was consumed by grief and fear, crying every night, and unable to sleep.

Obviously, the death of countless innocent civilians on both sides and the physical injuries that scores more have suffered as the result of the Israeli–Palestinian conflict have grabbed the attention of the public and the media. However, a less evident, but most disturbing and lasting, consequence of the protracted conflict between Israelis and Palestinians is the mental and emotional effect that it has on the survivors and witnesses of the violence. The most common psychological consequence of violence is posttraumatic stress, and in modern society, even in the relatively tranquil parts of the Western world, it is a somewhat common disorder. Normally, only about 5% of men and 10% of women develop fully diagnosed PTSD (posttraumatic stress disorder).[1] While the Associated Press reported in March 2005 that over 3,460 Palestinians and 1,025 Israelis had died since the resumption of hostilities and the outbreak of the Intifada in September 2000 (amongst them 514 Palestinian and 97 Israeli children under the age of 16), the number of *psychological* victims is not only many times greater but also very hard to assess. For instance, Devi[2] estimates that up to 60% of all Gaza's 1.3 million inhabitants show signs of posttraumatic stress but warns that the protracted conflict makes it very hard to use classic diagnostic assessment criteria. Similarly, Taubman-Ben-Ari and his colleagues[3] attempted to assess the prevalence of posttraumatic stress among Israelis by evaluating a random sample of about 3,000 primary care patients. These patients visited their physicians for a variety of ailments unrelated to psychological issues and therefore can be considered a representative sample of the population at large. Taubman-Ben-Ari found that over 23% of them reported experiencing traumatic events, and of those, about 39% met the criteria for PTSD.

What Is Posttraumatic Stress?

While we have known for a long time that experiencing trauma (i.e., terrible events outside the range of normal human experience) can have a negative effect on peoples' health and functioning, the formal definition of PTSD only dates from the late 70s and early 80s. Not until 1980 was the term PTSD first introduced by the American Psychiatric Association in the third edition of their *Diagnostic and Statistical Manual of Mental Disorders* (or DSM-III). Even then, the criteria for and definition of PTSD have not been totally agreed upon and have been modified numerous times in the past 26 years. As Rosenbaum[4] reports, there have been continuous changes in the definition of both the criteria needed to diagnose PTSD, as well as the length of time and the types of experiences that lead to it, between the 1980 DSM-III and the current version, the DSM-IV-TR (Text Revision).

In its present definition from the DSM-IV-TR, PTSD is classified as part of a group of mental disorders known as anxiety disorders, which are characterized by a heightened state of anxiety that impedes normal functioning of the person. Examples of other anxiety disorders include conditions such as phobias, in which a person suffers extreme anxiety because of a specific stimulus which is not logically threatening (like being in an elevator or on a high floor of a building). Another popularly well-known example is obsessive-compulsive disorder, in which the person is anxious about things like germs or organization and has the compulsion to clean up or arrange objects to alleviate the anxiety.

In short, the DSM-IV-TR explains that, in order to be diagnosed with PTSD, an individual needs to fulfill the following criteria:

A. Exposure to one major traumatic event *or* a history of events that involved death or injury (or the perception thereof).

B. A psychological reexperiencing of the event, for instance through persistent memories, dreams, feelings, hallucinations, or even physiological symptoms.

C. Efforts to avoid stimulus associated with the traumatic event, such as conversations, activities, people, or perceptual cues such as images or noises reminiscent of the event.

D. Increased arousal and hypervigilance, indicated for example by insomnia, irritability, oversensitivity, and difficulty concentrating.

E. These symptoms persist for at least one month, and

F. They impair the person's ability to function socially, occupationally, etc.

However, even though these might look like clear and straightforward criteria, the diagnosis of PTSD is not an easy one for a number of reasons. For example, one problem is that symptoms may appear only several months after a traumatic event is experienced. Another difficulty is that in some cases, the trauma can be induced not by being a direct witness of an event but by learning about an event (e.g., the death of a close relative) from other people or in some cases by just interpreting an event as threatening even if the actual event is not (e.g., a ride in an amusement park).

Which Factors Affect Posttraumatic Stress?

We all have experienced stress in our lives. Every time our daily routine gets out of balance, either as the result of daily hassles or as the result of major events, our body reacts by entering a heightened state of mental awareness and physical arousal to help us cope better with the changes. This physical and mental state is what we call *stress.*

Selye,[5] considered to be the father of modern stress research, suggested that stress moves forward in discrete stages as it becomes progressively more severe. First, in the alarm phase the "fight or flight" response is triggered and therefore the sympathetic nervous system gets activated in high gear. The whole body gets into a state of alarm. There are feelings of fear and/or excitement, with a physical spike of energy, as it prepares to either fight or flight.

If the stressors continue beyond the first stage, the body goes into the resistance phase. Because it cannot maintain such a high level of alertness, soon there is a drastic diminution of energy and a feeling of exhaustion. At this point, you begin to observe classical effects of stress such as disruption of sleep and appetite patterns, irritation, weakness, and other observable behavioral and physical changes.

Eventually, however, the body gets a feeling of fatigue, and the person moves into the exhaustion phase. The person gets totally worn out, and there can be a feeling of despair and helplessness. Physical symptoms include insomnia and severe weakness at the short term, and there are clear effects on the cardiovascular and the immune systems at the longer term.

The effects of stress can also vary significantly depending on the source, for example, if they are the result of common annoyances, such as traffic, bureaucracy, or work pressure, or when they come because of major, life-threatening situations. In general, the sources of stress, also known as *stressors,* are classified into three categories: (1) daily hassles, (2) major life changes, and (3) catastrophes. Daily hassles are small things that are irritating and annoying and for the most part can be expected to occur on a regular basis, such as, as we mentioned, traffic or work pressure. In the case of the Israeli–Palestinian conflict, it can also refer to things like Israeli checkpoints on the roads in the Palestinian territories or routine house searches by soldiers of IDF (Israel Defense Forces). On the Israeli side, it also refers to security checks in Israel, including metal detector scans, bag searches, and even body searches every time you enter a restaurant, a mall, or a supermarket. People are very resilient, and although these hassles provoke stress, they tend to adapt and with time learn to live with them, even though they have harmful chronic long-term health effects like heart disease or reduced functioning of the immune system.

The term "major life changes" refers to events that we will most likely experience throughout our lifetime, but they occur only rarely. Generally, they will also require us to make important changes in our daily lives. Some examples are the death of a spouse, relocation, loss of a job, divorce, and even marriage. Serving in the military or sending one's own children to serve are also major life changes in the Israeli and Palestinian societies, because in Israel military service is compulsory, and among the Palestinians, participating in actions against Israel as a teenager and a young adult is expected and socially required.

Finally, the last category, catastrophes, refers to severe threats outside the range of normal human experience that cause the perception of possible injury or death. These are the type of stressors we usually refer to when we talk about trauma, including things like major accidents, being victims of crime, natural disasters, and, certainly, war. Because of the extreme nature of these traumas, the effects of stress are so acute that they can cause physical and emotional symptoms that can impair the ability of a person to function normally in society, and thus, become PTSD.

It is important to mention that although there is a universal response to stress, every individual has a unique way of responding to stress-inducing catastrophic events. Some people are just more resilient, or stress-hardy, than others. Also, factors like social support, contextual circumstances, and even cognitive interpretations of the events can have an important impact on the extent of the trauma. However, during protracted conflict—as is the case of the Israeli–Palestinian one—in which both daily hassles and catastrophic events become common, we can expect levels of PTSD that are far higher than the norm in peaceful countries, with effects that go beyond the personal and into the social and cultural realms.

Posttraumatic Stress Among Palestinians

The Palestinian civilians living in the West Bank and Gaza Strip are probably among the world populations with the highest levels of stressors.

Not only do they face the daily hassles imposed by the Israeli occupation, such as numerous checkpoints, regular searches, and curfews, but they are also victims of economic deprivation, high levels of internal violence, and collateral damage of Israeli military operations. It is, therefore, not surprising to see that a number of studies have found very high levels of posttraumatic stress and other psychological disorders among Palestinians. For example, in July 2000, before the eruption of the current wave of violence and the Al-Aqsa Intifada, Zakrison, Shahen, and Mortaja[6] used the Rutter A2 test, a standard psychological test to measure emotional and behavioral problems, to test 203 children in eight randomly selected villages in a West Bank district. They discovered that a staggering 42% of children presented characteristics indicative of either psychological or behavioral problems. With the current wave of violence, the situation, as expected, seems to have become worse. In 2002, Qouta, Punamaki, and El Sarraj[7] assessed the level of PTSD and its correlation with exposure to traumatic events (e.g., shelling of a house) on a sample of 121 Palestinian children from the Gaza Strip. Their first finding was that a shocking percentage of children had been exposed to traumatic events, ranging from witnessed shootings (96%) to being teargassed (95%) to seeing a stranger being injured or killed (52%). The level of exposure to violence had a significant effect on the prevalence of posttraumatic stress, and Qouta and his colleagues found that more than half (54%) of the children presented severe levels of PTSD, over 33% had moderate levels, and 9% had mild levels. Only 1.7% of the children scored at a level in the PTSD scale that is indicative of no symptoms. Other similar studies have also found very high prevalence levels of PTSD in children in other areas of the Palestinian territories, like the 2005 study by Khamis,[8] who investigated East Jerusalem and West Bank children and found that a considerable percentage (55%) of children suffered a significant traumatic experience and that actual PTSD was diagnosed in over a third of them.

Of course, the effect of traumatic events go beyond the influence on children. The whole family structure is also affected. For example, in her book *Political Violence and the Palestinian Family: Implications for Mental Health and Well-Being,* Khamis[9] analyzes the effect of a number of politically related traumatic events (death or injury of a family member, having a family member imprisoned, and having their house demolished) on the mental health adjustment of the family unit. She studied 900 families, who had been victims of these traumatic events, both through quantitative questionnaires and through qualitative interviews and focus groups. Not surprisingly, Khamis found that exposure to this level of severe and protracted trauma was related to extremely high levels of adverse psychological outcomes, such as PTSD, anxiety, and depression. In addition, there was a major effect on family functioning. Traditional Palestinian families, with their strong patriarchal structure, were highly disrupted because of the big numbers of absent husbands and fathers, due to either death or prison or injury. Women not only were thrust into a position of tremendous responsibilities but also had to face diminished social and economic resources because of the absence or injury of their husbands. Children were forced into adult roles and in many cases traditional family functioning disintegrated. The normally strong family units typical of Arab and Muslim cultures weakened and gave way to radical political organization taking the role of shaping the youngsters' identity.

Another example of how this phenomenon affected family functioning among the Palestinians is a study conducted by Al-Krenawi, Graham, and Sehwail.[10] Al-Krenawi and his colleagues contacted the surviving relatives of the men who were killed in the 1994 Hebron massacre perpetrated by Baruch Goldstein (see Hate: The Psychology of Extremism, Dehumanization, and Violence) in order to study the bereavement responses and psychological effects of the trauma several years later. They were able to find twenty-three widows, twelve daughters, and twenty-six sons. They administered to all of them a standard instrument to assess broad symptoms of psychological distress in areas such as hostility, depression, anxiety, interpersonal sensitivity, obsessive-compulsive, and psychosis. Al-Krenawi and his colleagues found that even years after the traumatic events took place, surviving relatives of the dead presented elevated levels of somatization (physical symptoms with no medical cause associated with psychological trauma), anxiety, and phobias.

Giacaman and her colleagues[11] argue that the psychological effects of the occupation are hardly restricted to the higher incidence of mental disorders and elevated levels of stress, anxiety, or depression. Giacaman and her colleagues suggest that the whole social fabric and functioning of the community is impaired because of the combination of the destruction of infrastructure, severe economic limitations, and both the physical and the psychological health consequences. They conducted a comprehensive study in which they conducted a house-to-house survey of over 750 households living in five towns in a geographically diverse area of the West Bank that were invaded in 2002 by the IDF in a reaction to the *Al-Aqsa Intifada*. They concluded not only that they were able to document extensive damage to the infrastructure and the economy of the towns, greatly affecting the civilian population, but also that:

The social/health scale and subscales presented in this study clearly indicate that the effects of war on the civilian population go beyond physical damage of infrastructure, injury, death, and disability and have negative impacts on the life and health of survivors (p. 288).

In other words, it is clear that the effect of the many years of occupation by Israel of the Palestinian areas has had a cumulative psychological and social effect that will, in all likelihood, affect Palestinian individual and community mental health for the coming generation. The incredibly high level of exposure to traumatic events as well as the elevated levels of hassle-type stressors that are endemic to the Palestinian experience has caused a level of incidence of psychological disorders that is astounding and cannot be seen anymore as an abnormal condition within Palestinian society. We need, therefore, to be aware that when dealing with the Palestinians we are dealing with a society in which trauma, stress, and depression have become the norm rather than the exception, and that this fact has deep effects on their thinking, their culture, and their social interactions.

Posttraumatic Stress Among Israelis

Israel is a society of immigrants. Before the advent of Zionism, Palestinians formed a quite typical Arab culture, in which they had a strong attachment to the family land, their primary identification was with their extended clan, or *Hamula,* and agriculture was one of their main forms of sustenance. Unlike them, pre-Israel Jews were a very atypical nation, with few attachments to their birth lands, frequently rejected by the local nationals, and with a strong identification to a disperse nation and history. The long history of persecution, culminating in the Nazi Holocaust, created not only a culture of fear and distrust but also resiliency, which some authors have even compared to a "persecution complex."[12] What remains beyond doubt is that over half of the population of Israel was formed by either Holocaust survivors or refugees from countries where Jews had to escape either anti-Semitism or harsh economic conditions and that many of these immigrants arrived with already abnormal levels of posttraumatic symptoms and other psychological consequences of trauma. Many contemporary studies have found that, to this date, Holocaust survivors and even their children still suffer from the psychological consequences of trauma.[13] Other studies have shown high levels of psychological problems among immigrants both Ashkenazi, such as those from the former Soviet Union,[14] and Mizrahi, from the Middle East[15] and other non-Western countries like Ethiopia.[16]

To this background, you have to add the effects of a protracted state of war which started even before the 1948 war of independence, where almost 6,500 Jews were killed, amounting to nearly 1% of the Jewish population at the time of under 800,000. Since then, Israel has had a series of major wars and smaller conflicts with its Arab neighbors and has been under constant attack by irregular forces, like the Fedayeen in the fifties and sixties, the PLO in the seventies and eighties, Hezbollah in the eighties and nineties, and the two popular Palestinian uprisings, the *Intifada*, in the late eighties and early nineties and then in 2001 to 2005. This protracted state of conflict has had a very significant long-term effect on the individual and collective psyche of the Israeli people. An example among dozens of studies is the one by Shlosberg and Strous,[17] which followed up veterans diagnosed with PTSD after the Yom Kippur War of 1973. They reported that a total of 1,323 injured soldiers were referred for psychiatric evaluation during the war. Of those, 441 were diagnosed with various combat-related psychological disorders, 277 of them with what would be considered today PTSD. Shlosberg and Strous also found that even thirty-two years after the end of the war, nineteen veterans still suffered from PTSD.

On top of that sensitive background, the current situation of violence with the Palestinians has created a new generation of people affected by posttraumatic stress and other psychological disorders. Many studies have found high incidence of PTSD among Israeli children and adolescents.[18] One example is a study by Solomon and Lavi[19] that assessed a number of psychological variables, including PTSD, exposure to terror, orientation toward the future, and the future of peace talks, in 740 Jewish Israeli children (aged 11–15). These children were selected from areas that had been under violent attacks from the Palestinians, such as the Jerusalem neighborhood of Gilo (which during 2000–02 was under almost daily small arms fire from the Palestinian town of Beit Jala), or from Israeli settlements in the Palestinian territories. Solomon and Lavi found that children in all their sub-groups "were exposed to considerable terror-induced stress" (p. 1169) such as knowing somebody who had been killed or having been the target of a shooting or an attack. Furthermore, while all children reported higher than normal levels of posttraumatic stress, close to 30% of the Jewish children living in the occupied territories suffered from symptoms indicative of PTSD. Finally, it is important to note that Solomon and Lavi found that there is a significant correlation between exposure to violence and outcome variables such as negative future orientation and opposition to peace talks. In a different study, in 2001 Lavi[20] tested 1,300 Jewish Israeli and Palestinian children aged 13 to 15 and also found abnormally high levels of posttraumatic stress symptoms in all children, but specially among the Palestinian kids. A more recent study released by Mooli Lahad,[21] director of the Mashabim center of Tel Hai Academic College, in June of 2006, investigated the incidence of PTSD among residents of the town of Sderot, in southern Israel. The town has been the target for over three years of constant fire of the Kassam Palestinian rockets. The study found that about 50% of the parents and a third of the children are suffering from PTSD, and about 15% of the children suffer from severe levels of PTSD.

Exposure to traumatic events and posttraumatic stress symptoms also seem to be associated with more negative attitudes toward the enemy. For example, in one study, Laor, Wolmer, and Cohen[22] examined eighty-two Israeli families who were exposed to missile attacks during the 1991 Gulf War. First, Laor and his colleagues showed that children who showed posttraumatic symptoms also tended to have behavioral problems such as aggression, hyperactivity, and unpopular behaviors in school. More interestingly, however, severity of symptoms was closely related to a negative attitude toward Arabs. For example, of all children with severe symptoms, 66% reported a very negative attitude (e.g., "They are disgusting," "I hate them," and "I would like to kill them"), while 0% presented a balanced attitude (e.g., "Some of them are good, some of them are bad" and "We can not make generalizations"). In contrast, only 9% of children with mild symptoms showed a very negative attitude toward Arabs, while 26% showed a balanced one.

An illustrative paper related to the stress-related effects of the Israeli–Palestinian conflict among college students is presented by Shechtman.[23] She describes a session with graduate students in a counseling training program at a major Israeli university where 80% of the students were Jewish and 20% Arab Israelis. Shechtman reports her observations from the student discussions regarding the effects of the chronic (over time) and acute (intense) stress provoked by the conflict. Among other insights, the students talk about the sense of fear, the disruption of their normal lives and routines, and the negative attitudes that emerge from these feelings. Arab Israeli students in particular feel very distressed because, as Israelis, they are just as liable to be the targets of terrorist attacks, but as Arabs, they are also the target of prejudice and negative attitudes from Israeli Jews. Shechtman explains that as the conflict seems to amalgamate elements of both the acute and the chronic stressors, it has the effect of affecting long time attitudes and coping mechanisms in normal Israelis and has larger social effects.

Finally, the conflict has also had a stressful effect on Israelis who have served in the military and, essentially, have had to work in the repression of a civilian population instead of, as the basic IDF doctrine indicated, the defense against the attacks of an organized military force. This situation in which an organized military organization has to engage irregular forces is known as "asymmetrical encounters." For example, in one study, Maoz[24] interviewed twenty-two Israeli men who served in the IDF and were involved in actions aimed at suppressing the civilian uprising during the first Intifada in 1987–93. Maoz argues that when a conflict is asymmetrical and a vastly superior military force clashes against civilian populations, the soldiers have to cope with this imbalance with a number of psychological defense mechanisms that will justify their actions but at the same time have serious cognitive, emotional, and moral consequences. Maoz found that the soldiers could be classified into two groups: legitimizers, who fully justify their use of violence to suppress the uprising, and ambivalents, who compartmentalize their actions and without justifying them, see them as necessary but regrettable. The legitimizers suffered less psychological effects as the result of their actions; however, Maoz still found many negative consequences of their strategies such as a moral legitimization of the use of lethal force, dehumanization, prejudiced attitudes, alienation, and dissociation from their own actions. Among the ambivalents, the situation was far worse. Not only had they showed signs of trauma directly related to their actions during the military operations, such as guilt, shame, and regret, but the aftereffects of their asymmetrical encounters lasted well into their return to civilian life, where they describe instances of rage, moral ambivalence, and uneasiness normally associated with more severe trauma.

Another study that looks at the effects of the asymmetrical encounters between IDF soldiers and civilians was conducted by Dar, Kimhi, and

Stadler.[25] Dar and his colleagues interviewed 184 veterans of the IDF who were active during the first Intifada but were also members of the leftist kibbutz cooperative movement and had as a rule a very progressive, humanitarian education and values. Dar and his colleagues hypothesized that this contradiction had to lead to traumatic reactions, such as emotional anxiety, behavioral dilemmas, stress, and moral conflicts. While many of the veterans justified their experience as a way to give them better understanding of the conflict and the Palestinians, and even as strengthening their dovish attitudes and their criticism of the occupation, they still participated, to various extents, in the military actions against the civilians. They justified this participation by compartmentalizing and detaching their emotional beings from their soldier roles. Dar and his colleagues found, however, that in spite of the detachment and compartmentalization, the soldiers suffered "strong and deep" (p. 298) emotional effects and symptoms associated with posttraumatic stress such as fear, frustration, helplessness, pessimism, nightmares, and depression.

Other Psychological Consequences

Even though posttraumatic stress is the mental disorder most commonly associated with war and conflict, it is by no means its only psychological consequence. Several studies have looked at other effects of the Israeli–Palestinian conflict on mental health. For example, a study by Moore and Aweiss[26] examined over 3,700 Jewish, Arab Israeli, and Palestinian high school students to determine their perception of control and their sense of relative deprivation, concepts related to self-worth and self-image. Moore and Aweiss found negative effects among all students, but the Palestinian students fared worse, presenting the lowest sense of control, the highest feeling of personal deprivation, and the most negative expectations toward the future.

Also Slone, Adiri, and Arian[27] looked at psychological effects of negative "political events" among Israelis and Palestinians. These "political events" ranged from relatively mild, like exposure to political violence via the media and time spent in a bomb shelter, to more severe, like damage to property or injury or death of a friend or a family member. They conducted two studies, one comparing Israeli Jewish and Arab sixth and seventh graders and the second one comparing sixth grade Israelis and Palestinians. In the first, political events were correlated to the Brief Symptom Inventory, a scale that measures mental distress in areas such as obsessive-compulsive symptoms, interpersonal sensitivity, depression, anxiety, hostility, paranoid ideation, social alienation, etc. In the first study, Slone and his colleagues found a clear relation between exposure to negative political events and higher levels of psychological distress. The second study found that over 40% of Palestinian children have been exposed to severe negative political events. However, an interesting finding is that the Palestinian children who were more affected were those who had moderate levels of exposure, while those who had more severe levels of exposure seemed to have developed defense mechanisms that made them more resilient to the negative events.

One other area that was researched is the effect of political violence on the moral reasoning of children. A study conducted by Elbedour, Baker, and Charlesworth[28] looked at Jewish Israeli, Arab Israeli, and Palestinian elementary school children and attempted to determine if there was a relationship between exposure to political violence and the level of moral reasoning in children. The children were presented with both hypothetical and real-life moral dilemmas. Elbedour and his colleagues found not only that the Jewish Israeli children scored higher on moral reasoning than the Arab or Palestinian children in the real-life situations but also that for the boys in the sample, violence and economic deprivation directly affected the level of development of moral reasoning.

One final effect of political violence at a social and psychological level is the relationship it has with intersocietal violence. Landau[29] suggests that the legitimization of and habituation to violence that comes from political conflict result in an increase in internal violence. In addition, the heightened state of stress will also have a negative effect on internal violence. Although very little empirical research exists to confirm Landau's hypothesis, he reviews some literature that suggests a direct relationship between political violence in Israel and internal crime and violence against women. Similarly, Renna,[30] based on information gathered from his experience in counseling, believes that the recent increase in school violence in Israel is likewise related to the increase in political violence.

Among the Palestinians, the crisis on internal security is endemic. Armed gangs roam the streets with impudence and without fear of retribution, and crime levels are extremely high. Again, although empirical research is nonexistent, many commentators and analysts[31] have linked the deplorable internal security situation and the increase in family violence to the political conflict.

Prevention and Treatment

One final area that is worth touching when it comes to the psychology of conflict is the prevention and treatment of posttraumatic stress. Unlike PTSD caused by unforeseen traumatic experiences, such as accidents, violent crime, and rape, during protracted conflict mental health professionals can anticipate a psychological toll, can work on prevention strategies and interventions to minimize the damage, and can plan on treatment to become more efficient and resourceful at healing the mentally wounded. Paradoxically, mental health professionals both on the Palestinian and on the Israeli sides have become very proficient at doing just that and helping their respective populations become more resilient and re-adapt better and faster to normal life. However, because of the circumstances and the disparity of resources, there is obviously a lot more intervention and research on the Israeli side.

One example of the new challenges that mental health professionals had to overcome in this protracted conflict is presented in a paper by Wexler, Branski, and Kerem.[32] The authors are experienced mental health providers in the Israeli social health system, and as such, have provided and coordinated mental health services for Israelis and Palestinians for many years. They begin their paper by presenting an interesting notion that because the basic nature of modern war has developed from a traditional military confrontation between two armies and a somewhat definable front line to a more vague, protracted, low-intensity conflict, civilians tend to be more involved both in actual battle and in collateral damage. Wexler and his colleagues argue that because of the lower intensity and more chronic nature of modern conflicts, instead of the drastic changes in daily life that were usually the effect of traditional war, in this new type of conflict populations adapt and their routines and daily life are just modified, but largely maintained, which creates a challenge for health professionals who have to deal with a population that desperately wants to maintain a sense of normalcy. Furthermore, in the case of the Israeli–Palestinian conflict, they explain that the fact that in many areas the populations are intertwined and receive medical and mental health in the same locations makes it difficult for professionals to maintain the atmosphere of care and safety necessary to provide effective care. Wexler and his colleagues offer a number of suggestions they have learned from their experience. They suggest that "staff, at all levels, should be representative of the community it serves" (p. 1279), which means appropriate staffing of both Palestinian and Israeli professionals. Because of the multi-ethnic nature of the staff, Wexler and his colleagues suggest reducing sources of friction to a minimum, like prohibiting discussions about politics in premises, but organizing seminars and retreats to discuss and vent fractious issues. Another suggestion they make is related to language. Staff should have some proficiency in both languages, but the main care should ideally be delegated to a native speaker professional. They also suggest the use of nonverbal communication, especially with children.

Treatment and prevention of posttrauma becomes even more complex among Palestinians, not only because they have a higher stigma against mental health treatment, but also because of the barriers imposed by occupation and the inefficiency of the Palestinian authorities. In one report,[33] Eyad El-Sarraj, founder of the Gaza Community Mental Health Program, explains that not only are the infrastructure and government support insufficient but even the instruments and the research done in other parts of the world are inadequate. He has found that the use of volunteers has helped. Also, the emphasis on treatment within the family, which is more consistent with Palestinian cultural values, instead of hospitalization has had a positive effect, as well as integration of psychological therapies with Palestinian "traditional medicine" (banishing evil spirits and other superstitions), which helps the population accept the more psychological approach.

Other studies have found tremendous preventive value in classical stress-reduction factors such as family, social support, and romantic relationships. In one study, Demb[34] examined 453 Israeli adolescents and found that factors such as self-esteem, social support, family cohesion, and parental stress were related to resilience against stress in times of terror. In another article, Florian, Mikulincer, and Hirschberger[35] conduct three studies that look at the role of close romantic and personal relationships and their effect on terror-related stress. In all three studies they found that having a close romantic relationship helped cope with the fear of death, while having difficulties in personal relationships increased the level of stress.

There are also a number of studies that have dealt with the treatment of posttrauma among Israelis and Palestinians. Some studies point at the success of the use of brief coping techniques immediately following traumatic events, like a study done in Israel by Gidron and her colleagues,[36] who suggest a cognitive-based MSI (memory structuring intervention). MSI's goal is to change the processing of traumatic memories from the more nonconscious and uncontrolled affective processes in our mind to cognitive and linguistic processes that are controlled and can help us cope better with the perception of the events. Also Amir and her colleagues[37] describe the use of brief group psychotherapy in women exposed to terrorism as effective in preventing and reducing posttraumatic stress symptoms. More creative approaches have been studied, for example, by Josman and her colleagues[38] who conducted a number of studies on the use of virtual reality therapy using computers as helpful to threat victims of terrorism.

Long-term approaches have also been studied extensively in Israel. Foa[39] has reviewed the effectiveness of a number of psychosocial therapies to deal with the effect of conflict-related trauma, and Avrahami[40] has documented case studies of the success of visual arts therapy with victims of trauma in Israel.

However, it is a study by Quota, Punamaki, and El Sarraj[41] that offers the most obvious yet insightful glimpse at the best strategies to reduce posttraumatic stress. Quota and his colleagues examined the effect of the 1993 agreement between Israelis and Palestinians on the psychological well-being of the Palestinian children. They evaluated about seventy 11–12-year-old Palestinian children before and after the signing of the agreement. They found that the level of neuroticism of the children decreased in the months after the signing of the treaty. Furthermore, children who actively participated in the celebrations of the peace treaty showed improvements in self-esteem and showed even less neuroticism than those children who did not participate. Therefore, not only the positive perceptions of the treaty helped in overcoming the effects of trauma, embracing and supporting peace seemed to have an important effect too.

Chapter Conclusion

In summary, the impact of the protracted conflict on the mental well-being of both Palestinians and Israelis is unquestionable, especially in the children. Furthermore, because of the length of the conflict and its intrusiveness in all the spheres of life, its effects go way beyond the individual and into the social realm, where trauma and coping with it is becoming part of both the Israeli and the Palestinian cultures. Although there has been a lot of research done on techniques to provide more resiliency, to prevent the effects of trauma, and to help victims readapt to their normal lives, it is the last paper by Quota and his colleagues that provides the most insight into the problem. The solution to the social effects of posttrauma is not in the treatment, but in the removal of the trauma itself. Only after reconciliation, and only after several years of reconciliation, could we reverse the terrible effects of violence that leads us into our last chapter, which hopefully will be the most significant one of the book. Hope: Reconciliation and the Psychology of Peace.

Notes

1. Emily J. Ozer and Daniel S. Weiss, "Who Develops Posttraumatic Stress Disorder?" *Current Directions in Psychological Science* 13, no. 4 (2004): 169–72.

2. Sharmila Devi, "Protecting the Mental Health of Gaza's Inhabitants," *Lancet* 365, no. 9465 (2005): 1125–26.

3. O. Taubman-Ben-Ari, Jonathan Rabinowitz, and D. Feldman, "Post-Traumatic Stress Disorder in Primary-Care Settings: Prevalence and Physicians' Detection," *Psychological Medicine* 31, no. 3 (2001): 555–60.

4. L. Rosenbaum, "Post-Traumatic Stress Disorder: The Chameleon of Psychiatry," *Nordic Journal of Psychiatry* 58 (2004): 343–48.

5. H. Selye, *Stress in Health and Disease* (Boston, MA: Butterworths Inc., 1976).

6. Tanya L. Zakrison, Amira Shahen, and Shaban Mortaja, "The Prevalence of Psychological Morbidity in West Bank Palestinian Children," *Canadian Journal of Psychiatry* 49, no. 1 (2004): 60–63.

7. Samir Qouta, Raija-Leena Punamaki, and Eyad El Sarraj, "Prevalence and Determinants of PTSD Among Palestinian Children Exposed to Military Violence," *European Child & Adolescent Psychiatry* 12, no. 6 (2003): 265–72.

8. Vivian Khamis, "Post-Traumatic Stress Disorder Among School Age Palestinian Children," *Child Abuse & Neglect* 29, no. 1 (2005): 81–95.

9. Vivian Khamis, *Political Violence and the Palestinian Family: Implications for Mental Health and Well-Being* (Binghamton, NY: Haworth Maltreatment and Trauma Press/The Haworth Press, Inc., 2000).

10. Alean Al-Krenawi, John R. Graham, and Mahmud A. Sehwail, "Bereavement Responses Among Palestinian Widows, Daughters and Sons Following the Hebron Massacre," *Omega: Journal of Death and Dying* 44, no. 3 (2001–2002): 241–55.

11. Rita Giacaman and others, "Imprints on the Consciousness: The Impact on Palestinian Civilians of the Israeli Army Invasion of West Bank Towns," *European Journal of Public Health* 14, no. 3 (2004): 286–90.

12. For example, Nahum Goldmann, "The Psychology of Middle East Peace," *Foreign Affairs* 54, no. 1 (1975): 113–26; Louis Wirth, "Morale and Minority Groups," *American Journal of Sociology* 47, no. 3 (1941): 415–33.

13. For example, Motti Cohen, Danny Brom, and Haim Dasberg, "The Holocaust on Child Survivors and Children of Survivors," in "Child Survivors of the Holocaust: Symptoms and Coping After Fifty Years," *Israel Journal of Psychiatry and Related Sciences* 38, no. 1 (2001): 3–12; Natan P.F. Kellerman, "The Holocaust on Child Survivors and Children of Survivors," in "Psychopathology in Children of Holocaust Survivors: A Review of the Research Literature," *Israel Journal of Psychiatry and Related Sciences* 38, no. 1 (2001): 36–46; Yoram Bilu and Eliezer Witztum, "The Mental Health of Jews Outside and Inside Israel," in *Ethnicity, Immigration, and Psychopathology,* ed. Ihsan Al-Issa and Michel Tousignant (New York, NY: Plenum Press, 1997), 235–56.

14. Y. Lerner, J. Kertes, and N. Zilber, "Immigrants From the Former Soviet Union, 5 Years Post-Immigration to Israel: Adaptation and Risk Factors for Psychological Distress," *Psychological Medicine* 35, no. 12 (2005): 1805–14; A. Kamer, Ada H. Zohar, and R. Youngmann, "A Prevalence Estimate of Pervasive Developmental Disorder Among Immigrants to Israel and Israeli Natives: A File Review Study," *Social Psychiatry and Psychiatric Epidemiology* 39, no. 2 (2004): 141–45; A. Ponizovsky, Y. Ginath, and R. Durst, "Psychological Distress Among Ethiopian and Russian Jewish Immigrants to Israel: A Cross-Cultural Study," *International Journal of Social Psychiatry* 44, no. 1 (1998): 35–45.

15. Karen L. Pliskin, *Silent Boundaries: Cultural Constraints on Sickness and Diagnosis of Iranians in Israel* (New Haven, CT: Yale University Press, 1987), x, 283; A. Litman, I. Levav, and H. Saltz-Rennert, "The Use of Khat: An Epidemiological Study in Two Yemenite Villages in Israel," *Culture, Medicine and Psychiatry* 10, no. 4 (1986): 389–96; H.Z. Winnik, "Mibeayot hapsikhologia shel kelitat haäliya" [Psychological Problems of Immigrants Absorption], *Ofakim* 11 (1957): 138–44.

16. Rafael Youngmann, Sara Minuchin-Itzigsohn, and Miriam Barasch, "Manifestations of Emotional Distress Among Ethiopian Immigrants in Israel: Patient and Clinician Perspectives," *Transcultural Psychiatry* 36, no. 1 (1999): 45–63; A. Ponizovsky, Y. Ginath, and R. Durst, "Psychological Distress Among Ethiopian and Russian Jewish Immigrants to Israel: A Cross-Cultural Study," *International Journal of Social Psychiatry* 44, no. 1 (1998): 35–45.

17. A. Shlosberg and R.D. Strous, "Long-Term Follow-Up (32 Years) of PTSD in Israeli Yom Kippur War Veterans," *Journal of Nervous and Mental Disease* 193, no. 10 (2005): 693–96.

18. See, for example, Ruth Pat-Horenczyk, "The Trauma of Terrorism: Sharing Knowledge and Shared Care, An International Handbook," in "Post-Traumatic Distress in Israeli Adolescents Exposed to Ongoing Terrorism:

Selected Findings from School-Based Screenings in Jerusalem and Nearby Settlements," *Journal of Aggression, Maltreatment & Trauma* 9, no. 3–4 (2004): 335–47.

19. Zahava Solomon and Tamar Lavi, "Israeli Youth in the Second Intifada: PTSD and Future Orientation," *Journal of the American Academy of Child & Adolescent Psychiatry* 44, no. 11 (2005): 1167–75.

20. T. Lavi, "Yaldut beTzel haIntifada; Hashpaat haintifada al habriut hanafshit shel yeladim yehudim vepalestinaim" [Childhood in the Shadow of the Intifada: The Effect of the Intifada on the Mental Health of Jewish and Palestinian Children], Paper presented at the 2nd Bi-National conference on treating traumatized children and adolescents, Ma'ale Hachamisha, Israel. May, 2004.

21. Mooli Lahad, "Shlish Miyaldei Sderot Soblim mi post trauma" [A Third of Sderot Children Suffer of Post Trauma], Reported in the Web site of the Mashabim center: http://icspc.telhai.ac.il/

22. Nathaniel Laor, Leo Wolmer, and Donald J. Cohen, "Attitudes Toward Arabs of Israeli Children Exposed to Missile Attacks: The Role of Personality Functions," *Israel Journal of Psychiatry & Related Sciences* 41, no. 1 (2004): 23–32.

23. Zipora Shechtman, "Counseling and Building Communities of Peace," in "Stress in Israel: Voices in One Group Counseling Session of Counselor Trainees," *International Journal for the Advancement of Counselling* 25, no. 4 (2003): 247–53.

24. Ifat Maoz, "The Violent Asymmetrical Encounter With the Other in an Army-Civilian Clash: The Case of the Intifada," *Peace & Conflict: Journal of Peace Psychology* 7, no. 3 (2001): 243–63.

25. Yechezkel Dar, Shaul Kimhi, and Nurit Stadler, "Imprint of the Intifada: Response of Kibbutz Born Veterans to Military Service in the West Bank and Gaza," *Megamot* 39, no. 4 (1999): 420–44.

26. Dahlia Moore and Salem Aweiss, "Outcome Expectations in Prolonged Conflicts: Perceptions of Sense of Control and Relative Deprivation," *Sociological Inquiry* 73, no. 2 (2003): 190–211.

27. Michelle Slone, Michal Adiri, and Aviv Arian, "Adverse Political Events and Psychological Adjustment: Two Cross-Cultural Studies," *Journal of the American Academy of Child & Adolescent Psychiatry* 37, no. 10 (1998): 1058–69.

28. Salman Elbedour, Ahmad M. Baker, and William R. Charlesworth, "The Impact of Political Violence on Moral Reasoning in Children," *Child Abuse & Neglect* 21, no. 11 (1997): 1053–66.

29. Simha Landau, "Societal Costs of Political Violence: The Israeli Experience," *Palestine-Israel Journal of Politics, Economics and Culture* 10, no. 1 (2003): 28–35.

30. Bob Renna, "Israel and Palestine: Freedom and Survival in Their Holy Land," *International Journal of Reality Therapy* 19, no. 2 (2000): 24–28.

31. Sergio Herzog, "The Relationship Between Economic Hardship and Crime: The Case of Israel and the Palestinians," *Sociological Perspectives* 48, no. 2 (2005): 189–211; Anat Cohen, "Intifada Linked to Surge in Battering," *Herizons* 18, no. 2 (2004): 11.

32. Isaiah D. Wexler, David Branski, and Eitan Kerem, "Treatment of Sick Children During Low-Intensity Conflict," *Lancet* 365, no. 9466 (2005): 1778–79.

33. Sharmila Devi, "Protecting the Mental Health of Gaza's Inhabitants," *Lancet* 365, no. 9465 (2005): 1125–26.

34. Meira Demb, "Resilience in a Time of Terror: Individual, Social, and Familial Protective Factors in Israeli Adolescents," *Dissertation Abstracts International: Section B: The Sciences and Engineering* 66, no. 7-B (2006): 3944.

35. V. Florian, M. Mikulincer, and G. Hirschberger, "The Anxiety-Buffering Function of Close Relationships: Evidence That Relationship Commitment Acts as a Terror Management Mechanism," *Journal of Personality and Social Psychology* 82, no. 4 (2002): 527–42.

36. Y. Gidron and others, "Translating Research Findings to PTSD Prevention: Results of a Randomized-Controlled Pilot Study," *Journal of Traumatic Stress* 14, no. 4 (2001): 773–80.

37. M. Amir and others, "Debriefing with Brief Group Psychotherapy in a Homogenous Group of Non-Injured Victims of a Terrorist Attack: A Prospective Study," *Acta Psychiatrica Scandinavica* 98, no. 3 (1998): 237–42.

38. Naomi Josman, Eli Somer, and Ayelet Reisberg, "Virtual and Physical Toys: Open-Ended Features for Non-Formal Learning," in "Designing a Virtual Environment for Post-Traumatic Stress Disorder in Israel: A Protocol," *CyberPsychology & Behavior* 9, no. 2 (2006): 241–44.

39. E.B. Foa, "Psychosocial Therapy for Posttraumatic Stress Disorder," *Journal of Clinical Psychiatry* 67, Suppl. 2 (2006): 40–45.

40. D. Avrahami, "Visual Art Therapy's Unique Contribution in the Treatment of Post-Traumatic Stress Disorders," *Journal of Trauma & Dissociation: The Official Journal of the International Society for the Study of Dissociation (ISSD)* 6, no. 4 (2005): 5–38.

41. Samir Qouta, Raija-Leena Punamaki, and Eyad El Sarraj, "The Impact of the Peace Treaty on Psychological Well-Being: A Follow-Up Study of Palestinian Children," *Child Abuse & Neglect* 19, no. 10 (1995): 1197–208.

INTERVIEWS

An Interview with Ron, Who Lives in Northern Israel. Interviewer: Amir Hermosa

Ron (fictitious name) is 36 years old, married with a toddler son. By occupation Ron is a yoga teacher in the northern region. Ron experienced a traumatic event and survived it.

Interviewer: Hello Ron, how was the trip coming here? I was stuck in many traffic jams on the way, and the excitement did not add to my tolerance.

Ron: Yes, I have also come from the southern direction. I had difficulty finding a parking place, but here I am, and it is a nice place. Shall we order something to drink? I would like to have a cup of coffee.

Interviewer: I would have a cup of herbal tea. OK, tell me a little about yourself.

Ron: Where do I begin? OK, I'm Ron. I'm 36 years old, and father to a little boy of 1.5 years old. I'm very happy to be a father, although I've found out that I have an over-anxiousness, and my wife claims all the time that she discovers the "Polish" aspect in me, although my family comes from Turkey. (The characteristics of the Polish mother in Israel signify, among other things, an over protecting mother). I'm in the yoga business, that is, I'm a yoga teacher, a therapist through movement, and... (censored).

Interviewer: What do you love to do, except from being a father?

Ron: I love traveling, and do sports, not a challenging sport, but more personal. I love to read, to listen to good music, and there is one more important thing, my friends say I love to laugh.

Interviewer: Let's go a little bit inside toward the level for which we have met today. I understand that you were a victim of the conflict between us and our neighbors, and I understand that it is difficult for you to talk about it, but let's try to make one step together toward this event. Can you tell me a little of what happened?

Ron: I was sitting in a café, a regular day. It was very nice and I was talking to a friend, when suddenly, on the other side of the street a powerful explosion was heard (silence).

Interviewer: May I offer you a cup of water?

Ron: Thank you, and then there was a feeling, that is hard to describe in words, of nonexistence, as if everything stopped being. It was a matter of some hundredths of a second, but I lost the sense of time and it looked like eternity for me.

Interviewer: What do you remember from these moments?

Ron: I don't remember exactly what was there. I only remember my feeling at that long minute, five years ago, and at that moment I felt the blood stopped flowing to my face, and all I felt was a feeling of sweat and suffering that is hard to describe, you can only feel it deep inside.

Interviewer: Let's try to reconstruct that moment after the explosion regarding what happened around you.

Ron: There was a boom, and then silence, and right after the silence, there were weak cries for help, which is hard for me to forget even today! And then there was the noise of the sirens and car horns blowing, and noise and a tumult at the same time coming to me.

Interviewer: How have you got injured in this event?

Ron: My injury was from pieces of glass, which flew toward me, and I was lucky as I was hiding my face instinctively with my other arm. Otherwise, I would have gotten the pieces of the shock wave, so the severe injury was the psychological injury that was discovered only afterward.

Interviewer: I feel it is very difficult for you, but I'm very much interested, not as a student but as a person, to hear you, and I would be very glad if you could go on telling me, if it is OK with you, a little about the inner event you have gone through.

Ron: After I have been taken to the hospital, where I was treated, and later on released, I came home and thought that it was all over. I have told my family members about the event. All of them have been very anxious and cared a lot for me. One may say that they have all been exploded, but from anxiety. I couldn't fall asleep at nights, I heard the boom again and again, and every door that slammed added a significant number to my blood pressure. I became a very intolerant person, and I used to become nervous for any nonsense. I would yell at my sister and my family members, and at night I used to find myself wide-awake for many hours. I used to go back to the place of the event, trying to understand.

Interviewer: What did you try to understand?

Ron: I tried to understand something that has not been clear to me until today (long silence). Why actually do they hate us?

Interviewer: And have you got an answer?

Ron: Because this is their culture, or more correctly, this is the culture they distort and believe in their distortion, that it is their task to destroy us.

Interviewer: How did the event influence you?

Ron: I came to be a very closed person within my own world, and I refused to go out to have a good time. I think that because I couldn't do the separation from the event to everyday life, the event haunted me, do you understand?

Interviewer: What you are telling me is something very powerful, and I have no words to try to describe my feelings toward your pain. Have you felt a need to go to talk to someone?

Ron: At first no, but very quickly I have understood that I had to, and today it is easier for me because of this. I used to meet a professional, and he helped me understanding what, why, and especially how one can go on living in this exploding country.

Interviewer: Do you feel that you still carry things from this event?

Ron: Look, there is no doubt that today, five years after those feelings, the fears have diminished, although the sights and the sounds are still there since that event, and the help I have got also helped me a lot, but to answer your question, yes, today I also become highly panicked when I hear a door being slammed, or a sudden noise of an airplane. In days when there is a terrorist attack I feel so bad that I even can't tell you how anger comes up and accumulates in my stomach, and I feel bad.

Interviewer: Has the event influenced you in other ways—economically, socially...?

Ron: Sure, during the year of the event, I couldn't concentrate at work, although I had a strong need to go on forward, since I said that if God wanted me to stay alive, and I stayed alive, then I must be strong. But there was the gap, I'll not lie to you and say that I have returned to work like a tiger! It was difficult, but the event, as you call it, was a turning point in my life in the mental and the spiritual level. I don't mean that I have gone back to be religious, but since then an awful lot of things have become clearer to me.

Interviewer: Can you try to be more specific?

Ron: Look, as I have said, if God would have wanted me to die, I would have gone. But the very fact that I survived means that I have stayed here in order to be stronger, to try to understand the meanings of things better. Look, by nature I'm a very spiritual person, and I think that all my being and goal have been sharpened.

Interviewer: How is it being expressed today?

Ron: I ask more questions, I try to be more thorough, and you know what, I have also been strengthened psychologically. Thank God, I have found a wife, and I have a son, and sometimes it is difficult for me, but the spiritual levels help the materialistic levels.

Interviewer: Let me take you back to the Israeli–Palestinian conflict, what do you think of it?

Ron: Good question. Look, basically I am a man of peace, and my spiritual point of view is spiritual as well. But the things that happen here in Israel prove us everyday that we have no one to talk to. Don't forget that there was no such thing, which was called Palestinians before the establishment of the State of Israel, and we have been here before them. And besides, we are willing to give them. Look how Sharon gave them, and today we received machinegun fire in Ashkelon. You see that the leftists live in illusions. They (the Arabs) understand only strength, and that's it.

Interviewer: So do you think that by strength only we will solve the conflict? Will we kill one another until the end?

Ron: You don't understand! It is a matter of deterrence. After the Six-Day War they have been quiet. Why? Because they understood that we were stronger, but today they allow themselves to do severe things, like terrorist attacks, because they think that we have weakened. You should understand their thinking! I, too, said all the time "peace, peace."

Interviewer: And you feel that the event has actually changed you political point of view?

Ron: To a large extent yes, I think. It is sad to say, but the fear and the anger have taken the room of compassion.

Interviewer: Can you be more specific?

Ron: I mean that if beforehand I had given a chance to different kinds of behaviors, and I had loved being one day in the left and the next in the right, today my point of view is very obvious!

Interviewer: And what is it?

Ron: Until they don't stop the cycle of violence on their part, there is no one to talk to. And if they play power struggles, we have to do the same, to be more determined!

Interviewer: That means that for every explosion in a bus, you should explode a town. Does it sound sensible to you, as you claim that you are a very spiritual person and so on?

Ron: Look, even in the world of the Bible it is written: "If someone comes to kill you, kill him first." Whoever doesn't know to keep the lives of his children, has no meaning in the world. I speak about very high levels of values of war and peace. They don't understand at the moment, in their level of development, nothing but power—to shoot a bus full of children on its way to school, what a level is it?

Interviewer: Ron, don't you think that you generalize. There are some who are interested in blowing up the whole process, and they want you to think that they represent everybody!

Ron: I used to talk just like you. You are simply naïve, if you think that those who see and don't report are not accomplices of the crime. And besides, what about the leadership? All the Palestinians are the extension, which executes the theory of the Arab world, who doesn't want us to be here. For they claim, listen to what the Iranian lunatic has said: that we would be returned to Europe! Do you start getting what is going on here?

Interviewer: So you think that we would not manage to solve the conflict between us?

Ron: No, or more correctly, maybe in the future either they would understand that we are here forever, or they would not be here.

Interviewer: But all the same, let's be a little clearer?

Ron: Look, as long as they don't understand that we are here as a people, and it is our right, there is no one to talk to. Secondly, if their government continues being full of Hamasniks and criminals, nothing will move, and even if they don't start bringing some order in there and stop talking in two voices, one that supports the annihilation of Israel, the Zionist enemy, and the other that says that one has to make peace—we have no partner. They want us both to get out of the territories, pay them national security, let them steal cars, and that we will accept the murdering of innocent civilians!

Interviewer: But try to look on it from the eyes of the simple Palestinian, who wants food and work.

Ron: Food, work, and that Jews be annihilated as well! I feel no pain for him. Let them make a revolution and expel the corrupt people, like other revolutions have done all over the world, let them see to it that they have a regime which provides them with salaries, and doesn't take the assistance money, like Yasser Arafat did, let his name be obliterated!

Interviewer: What is the solution in your opinion? We can't live here as people are killed all the time. The young people of today are not like those in the past. They look for convenience, they want a country that helps and not put most of its money on security?

Ron: Look, whoever doesn't want to be here and understand this complicated life system, let him go. We are not Europe, where, by the way, there have been wars and revolutions for almost two hundred years. We see their final product today.

Interviewer: Yes, but who wants to wait for two hundred years?

Ron: This is the point, Amir, you have to sow so that your grandchildren will harvest.

Interviewer: Harvest what, seeds of war?

Ron: Maybe until then they will understand the facts we have been talking about along the way. Don't forget that we have also gone a long way, and today we give them an existence like a state. They just have to organize themselves and stop the nonsense and understand a few insights, which will make them a nation.

Interviewer: And we don't have to crystallize an arranged policy? We, too, have to calm down all sorts of crazy forces in our camp, who threaten the existence of our regime, like the Feiglins and others.

Ron: That is correct, but don't forget that we are the chosen people; this land was destined for us. For two thousand years we have studied and studied and wandered, we are busy with self-guilt, but they are busy half of the time by expelling us. Look how they slaughtered us along the history. I say that we just have to be careful of them.

Interviewer: So what is the solution, we will be careful about them, and they about us, we will get exploded and they will put bombs again and again?

Ron: Look, I don't have a solution, like anyone else doesn't. I know that as far as we are concerned, we have no other place to go to, and we are ready to live with our neighbors according to our conditions and compromises, or else, we will all live on our swords.

Interviewer: Would you like to add something, as we have to finish our formal conversation.

Ron: I hope that people would not experience what I have experienced. But there is someone who guards on us, and we have to be more attentive and strong.

Interviewer: Thank you.

An Interview with Ibrahim, Who Lives in the West Bank, in the Palestinian Territories. Interviewer: Jacqueline Abu Alhija

Ibrahim is a 38-year-old man and a young father to his family. By occupation Ibrahim is an electrician and although today he works mostly in the Palestinian territories, he used to work in Israel and have daily contact with Israelis. Ibrahim experienced a traumatic event when several members of his immediate family were killed in an Israeli air strike.

Interviewer: Hello.

Ibrahim: Hello to you too.

Interviewer: Before we begin talking about the main topic, can you tell me a little about yourself?

Ibrahim: What would you like to know? Hmm . . . my name is Ibrahim, I'm 38 years old, I live in a small town in the country of Palestine, of course, I rather not say the name of the town.

Interviewer: What is your occupation?

Ibrahim: I am an electrician, I deal with home systems, industrial systems, most of my work is odd jobs inside Palestine. I also have a permit that I must renew every three months and must pay 3,500 shekel (about $800 US dollars) so I can work in Israel.

Interviewer: I understand that you were a victim of the Palestinian–Israeli conflict, and I really appreciate that you are willing to participate because I know how hard and painful it is to talk about it.

Ibrahim: Don't worry, I am used to the pain and the sorrow, and as they say, I almost lost all my feelings.

Interviewer: I apologize if I am opening painful . . .

Ibrahim: Don't worry, feel free, I really want to help you in this project, and I wish you are successful.

Interviewer: Thank you. Can you tell me a little bit of what happened then?

Ibrahim: I'll tell you, why not. I am a victim of the conflict, and I think not only me, but my all family, and there are many others like us. Specifically, what happened to me and my family was that . . . ahh . . . we could say injuries in a number of areas that we all were hurt in: the first injury is less important, the economic damage, and that is that my house was destroyed, my parents' house, and we did not have a place to sleep for three months. And I don't have money to build even one room. For the first three months after the incident, I had to borrow some money from a friend to build a small house, but to this day it doesn't have a floor or finished walls. And until now, even after five years, I have not had been able to repay the money to my friend. I believe that you can understand the feeling of all of us living for about ten years in a house of less than 100 square meters (about 900 square feet). And let's not forget the most painful thing for all of us, who were under the rubble of the house after it was destroyed. First, it was my little brother, who used to live with my mom and my dad, but also, what I will never forget in all my life and I remember every minute, it was my son. And this hurts more than a hundred times more than having the house destroyed, and to this day the pain and the sorrow don't leave the door of our house.

Interviewer: I understand how painful this can be for you and your family...Can you explain to me how this painful incident affected you?

Ibrahim: Ahh...The truth is that it affected me very much both psychologically and in my health. After the incident, I always felt like being strangled, without energy, helpless, and also anxious for the family. I worry more and more every time. I'm constantly worried and apprehensive that an incident like this will happen again.

Interviewer: So what is your opinion about the conflict?

Ibrahim: In my opinion this is something that is unavoidable, because there is a basic problem that cannot be resolved easily. When I start to think about it by myself, I have these thoughts about different possibilities related to this problem. Sometimes, when I am calmed, I think that this is harming both countries and we have to once and for all stop to add more pain and sorrow to both peoples. Because it is only the people who have to pay the price. But sometimes, when I think about my story, and how the same thing happens to more and more persons from my people, then I don't care about anybody around me and all I can think of is revenge.

Interviewer: Have you experienced a change in your opinion regarding the conflict before and after the incident that happened to you?

Ibrahim: Before the incident, my thoughts were around a solution to the problem and how we could live in peace. Especially because my town is really close to the State of Israel. I used to work most of the time in the State of Israel, and most of the time I used to be there and I had many friends that I used to work with, so why not to have a shared existence without problems and conflicts? But afterward...hmm...what can you expect from a person who lost so many important things in his life. And don't say that God took them, it was the Israelis that took them from us. What do you think is my feeling toward the State of Israel? Only hatred.

Interviewer: As we all know, this conflict has been going on for many years already. Why do you think we have not found a solution for it?

Ibrahim: In my opinion the problem is really huge because the conflict is a problem of the whole nation. It is not like a conflict between two persons. There are many different opinions between the two nations and at the end it is very difficult that one of them will give up, even a small thing, and every side wants everything. And that is what is happening on the field. The strong side feels that it has the power and it can take whatever it wants, the weaker side fights on and doesn't give up. On the other hand I feel that there are many other sides that are involved, directly or indirectly, like other countries that do not want the conflict to end. You see, if you ask me, in my view the world today is like a jungle, the strongest eats the weakest. But even I feel that even if the country of Palestine were to receive what it wanted, I don't think that the conflict will end because there are many people that will not be satisfied with a solution, they just want vengeance because of what was done to them. In my view the conflict has become one of hatred from both sides. And also on our side, there have been many things done that we don't publicize in the media...And this thing really upsets me, nobody really knows what is going on in the state of Palestine, the media doesn't report everything, and when they do report it, the Israelis for sure will manipulate it and turn it around to support their point of view.

Interviewer: Can you give me an example that the things that are not reported in the media?

Ibrahim: There are people who are seeing in front of their noses how people rape their mothers or their sisters or their daughters, in front of their noses, or how they are hitting children and elderly people, and the men can't do anything about it. How they kill the relatives in front of a father, or a son...This has caused the problem to just get worst, it is not limited anymore to issues of a country, territory, or land. Instead, it has turned into many personal conflicts where everybody wants to recover their honor, and avenge what they saw. Therefore, I cannot see any short-term solution and the problem will only grow bigger...Another point that I didn't relate to is that the Palestine country is a country where faith and religion are very important, contrary from the State of Israel. Therefore, the religious conflict also comes in, and about that issue you can fight to the end of time because so much faith is such an important thing in the state of Palestine, and the problem is that Israel pushes these issues on purpose, because it doesn't respect what we believe in.

Interviewer: So you feel that you want to seek vengeance against Israel after the incident that happened to you?

Ibrahim: I prefer to keep my feelings inside me. What I can tell you is that I will never forget.

Interviewer: What do you think will be the solution at the end?

Ibrahim: As I said, the solution will not be easy at all, and the conflict will continue forever. There will be a total war, and the situation will continue until one of the countries disappears. Or there is one other solution, but it is really unlikely, that the large countries will force Israel to sign and agree with international law.

Interviewer: And which one of these solutions is more likely?

Ibrahim: The truth is that I think that the situation will deteriorate to total war, but if it doesn't, I am sure that the Palestinians will not accept anything else easily.

Interviewer: Is there anything else you would like to add?

Ibrahim: What I would like to add is that my people are like any other people in the world, and not like the Israelis think. I heard many Israelis who say that we don't value ourselves and that we don't value our babies. Everything that is said until now is incorrect, we do value those things and even more than them. What we did, we did out of lack of choices. What can you expect from a person whose mother and whose father and whose brother and whose sister was crushed under their house or a father whose son was killed while being held by his father's arms.

What can he find in life? And there are many people like that. It is impossible to empathize with them, only, god forbid, if you are in their place. But at the end everybody wants a life of peace and to live with their families without fear and worries that we will not survive until tomorrow, or that you will lose a dear person every hour. We only live day-by-day and we have no dreams anymore, no expectations, just enough pain for everybody.

Interviewer:　　Thank you very much. I do hope that your anxiety and your pain will end soon and that peace and a normal life will come back for everybody. I really thank you and wish you a good and quiet life. Thanks.

Ibrahim:　　You're welcome.

HOPE: RECONCILIATION AND THE PSYCHOLOGY OF PEACE

I like to believe that people in the long run are going to do more to promote peace than our governments. Indeed, I think that people want peace so much that one of these days governments had better get out of the way and let them have it.

Dwight D. Eisenhower, American President

Kibbutz Metzer is a cooperative agricultural community located in the border with the Palestinian territories. The kibbutz, founded in 1953 by members of the leftist "HaShomer HaTzair" youth movement, has been for the past fifty years at the forefront of the Israeli peace camp. They developed a one-of-a-kind collaborative relationship with their former enemies in the Israeli Arab village of Meisir and fought against the route of the separation fence, so, at the expense of their own lands, it does not annex Palestinian lands. They promoted many other coexistence projects between Israelis and Palestinians, fueling the dream of peace. Then, on November 10, 2002, a Palestinian gunman, seeking to shatter those dreams, infiltrated the kibbutz. First, he killed the general secretary, Yitzhak Dori, who was performing guard duty that night, and then entered one of the houses, gunning down point-blank a young woman, Revital Ohayoun, and her two little children, Matan, aged 5 and Noam, aged 4.

These brutal and cold-blooded murders should have been enough to kill the dreams of the members of two communities: the Jewish Socialists in Metzer, who passionately believed in peace and coexistence, and the Palestinian Israeli inhabitants of Meisir, who had prided in their unique relationship with the kibbutz, with whom they had the only joint Jewish-Arab professional soccer team and whose swimming pool is always open to the children of Meisir. But it did not. Reportedly, right after the killings, the gunman, ironically named Sirhan Sirhan, tried to escape through the Arab town, but the locals blocked his route and even helped track him down on his way back to the Palestinian territories. And according to the British paper the *Guardian,*[1] a delegation from the Arab village immediately went to Metzer to express its solidarity. Tahir Arda, leader of the delegation, said that "We are one family, Metzer and Meisir" and explained how he even volunteered in 1967 to work on the fields of the kibbutz: "when the kibbutz men went to war for Israel...I drove the tractor on Metzer."

On the Israeli side, Metzer residents, although deeply shaken, were also mostly undeterred by the attack. They were determined to press forward with their peace and coexistence projects. As reported in the *Guardian,* the kibbutz treasurer, Dov Avital, said that "They (the attackers) wanted to show there is no such thing as coexistence. They think Palestinians should fight Jews. If they kill our dream, our vision of life, then they will have succeeded." Even in their moment of grief, kibbutz members actually took advantage of the condolence visit of then Prime Minister Ariel Sharon to reiterate their request that the separation fence be moved inside the Israeli pre-1967 borders and spare the fields of the Palestinian villagers of Qafin, just across the border.

Today, nearly 4 years after the attack, Metzer and Meisir are still a model of coexistence. They used the lessons they learned from the terrorist attack to create a program for visitors, to teach about coexistence, to further mutual Arab–Israeli experiences for the youth, and to promote joint ventures between Israeli Jews and Arabs and even between Israelis and Palestinians. Needless to say, if that spirit of cooperation and resilience were typical of the Israelis and the Palestinians, the conflict would have been resolved many years ago. What makes them different? What are the processes and the characteristics that allowed these former enemies to become partners and allies? How can you reach that level of dialogue and understanding?

Psychology of Negotiations

You could argue that in order to be able to have social coexistence, first you need to reach political understanding and agreements. And the first step toward political peace and reconciliation is, of course, negotiations. However, in order to be able to have dialogue and reach agreement, it is important that communication be clear and the construction of meaning be similar by both parties. Unfortunately, this is the first obstacle in any Arab–Israeli dialogue. Israeli and Palestinian communication styles, with their respectively Western and Middle Eastern influences, could hardly be more different. For example, according to a review of the research by Feghali,[2] Arab communication patterns are marked by constant repetition, indirectness, and elaborateness. Arabs in general tend to be highly contextual, reading "between the lines," rather than literal in their speech and writings, and with a style that is intricate and complex. In contrast, Western style of communication is direct, concerned with efficiency, concise, and context independent.[3] Indeed, these huge differences in communication styles have been reported to be the source of a number of diplomatic conflicts between Arabs and Westerners.[4] For instance, it is widely reported that before the 1991 Gulf War, the statement by U.S. Ambassador to Iraq April Gillespie to Saddam Hussein, "We have no opinion on the Arab-Arab conflicts, like your border disagreement with Kuwait," was actually interpreted by Hussein as meaning "we will not intervene if you attack them," and therefore Hussein saw it as a green light to invade Kuwait.

More specifically, the Israeli and Palestinian communication styles have been studied by Katriel.[5] He has identified the Palestinian communication style as *musayra,* which literally means "to accommodate." It is a communication style whose purpose is more agreeable social relations and a concern for honor and respect for the addressee. It is indeed indirect, repetitive, elaborate, and emotional. In contrast, Katriel identifies the Israeli communication style as *dugri,* which literally means "straight talk," and is designed to be concise, effective, direct, and pragmatic. Can these differences between the *musayra* and the *dugri* styles of communication be the source of misunderstanding also between Israelis and Palestinians? A number of researchers have analyzed the effect of these communication patterns on Israeli–Palestinian relationships. For example, Ellis and Maoz[6] investigated specifically if these differences in communication style are present in small group Palestinian–Israeli dialogue. They collected data on a large number of Israeli–Palestinian small group exchanges and found that indeed the cultural communication styles did affect dialogue. However, they also found that the effect of communication patterns was not as strong as the effect of the power differential between the minority and the majority status of the groups. Researchers Manusov and Milstein[7] looked instead at mass media effects and reported that cultural differences also affect how both mass media and the public end up with different interpretations of nonverbal language messages, such as the Rabin–Arafat handshake. Interpretations of the handshake varied widely. It was largely identified as a somewhat vague sign of hope, but in some cases, depending on the political orientation of the observer, more as a firm agreement (more typical of some Israelis), and in other cases even as a betrayal (more typical of some Palestinians). The same principle of cultural interpretation can be inferred with other media events such as public speeches or official declarations, which are more than likely interpreted very differently by the source group than by the target. Donohue[8] even analyzed the process that led to the Oslo peace process, and he found that ambiguity of purpose and language, a concept he calls equivocality, was one of the major obstacles that had to be overcome in order to achieve an agreement.

Communication style differences are certainly a variable that has to be taken into consideration when conducting more formal, diplomatic dialogue and negotiations, but they are not the only one. Psychological research has shown that when conducting negotiations, the rational, pragmatic issues on the table are not by far the only factors affecting the outcome of negotiations. Rather, as the research by Katriel already suggested, psychological issues such as the perception of power and fairness play an even greater role in the willingness of each side to accept a solution.

For example, an important factor affecting successful dialogue has to do with subjective expectations and perceptions of the negotiation process and results. One of the most studied phenomena affecting the outcome of negotiations between conflicting groups is the notion of *procedural justice.* In other words, in order for the two parties to be able to achieve a positive outcome from negotiations, they have to *perceive* that the process of negotiation was fair, consistent, and impartial. Research has shown that with an identical situation, negotiators are more likely to reject a proposal if they perceive that the process was not just (for instance, if they believe a mediator is not impartial or that the opposing party has a hidden agenda) than if the exact same proposal is presented when there is a perception of fairness in the process.[9] Another important factor is *distributive justice,* the perception that the allocation of the disputed resources resulted in a fair outcome. Many factors can affect the perception of distributive justice, but the expectation of the outcome is a good illustrative example of one important influence. If, for instance, the original expectation of a party was that they would receive 75% of the disputed resources and a proposal that is rationally fair suggests dividing the resource 50–50, the affected party might perceive this outcome as unfair because its original expectations were different.[10]

How do the perceptions of procedural and distributive justice affect Israeli–Palestinian negotiations? Apparently, Israelis and Palestinians have very different perceptions of who would be an adequate mediator that can help the perception of procedural justice. One study that looks into this question was conducted by Hare, Ashhab, and Kressel,[11] who in 2001 (after the beginning of the Intifada) surveyed about three hundred Israeli and Palestinian students as well as Israeli professionals involved in mediation activities. They found that although both sides agreed that a mediator should be task oriented, Israelis expect the ideal mediator to be more friendly, that is, to have characteristics such as sociable, likable, and trustful. Somebody who is perceived by the Israelis as friendly is unlikely to be perceived by the Palestinians as impartial. Consequently, a mediator who can bring a sense of procedural justice to the Israeli side will in fact be perceived as biased by the Palestinians, and vice versa. One needs no more than to think of the role of the United States, who is the preferred mediator to Israelis, but who the Palestinians actually deeply distrust. In another study, Schrodt and Gerner[12] studied actual mediation efforts related to the Israeli–Lebanese conflict and eventual cease fire and the Israeli–Palestinian peace initiatives after the first Intifada, from 1979 to 1999. Schrodt and Gerner created a matrix based on news reports of mediation efforts by the United States, the United Nations, and the European Union and then followed the time line to correlate the effects of the different efforts. Although their analysis methods are very complex, some more apparent conclusions can be drawn from their study. First, mediation efforts between Israelis and Palestinians have been successful in reducing the level of conflict, specially when accompanied by tangible material "stick and carrot" (sanctions and rewards) incentives and material cooperation with the weaker side. Second, mediation efforts by the United States are hard to assess because of "the close relationship between Israel and the United States" (p. 225) that makes their mediation initiatives more complicated.

Mishal and Morag[13] argue that the negotiating styles and expectations of Arabs and Israelis are affected by their cultures and social structures and therefore are themselves very different. Mishal and Morag explain that whereas the Israelis have a more Western style "hierarchical" social structure, the different Arab parties tend to have a more "networked" one, and that this difference affects both the negotiation process and the expectations they have. According to the authors, the hierarchical structure is characterized by vertical relations between the state and the people, clear rules and expectations, and strong identification with the state and more formal procedures. In contrast, networked structures are more fragmented and sectorial, with a fluid and varied level of identification with the state and government, and the legitimacy of the state is constantly negotiated according to more ambiguous rules and a balance of power between the different sectors. These differences lead the more hierarchical Israelis to be goal oriented in their negotiations and expect a firm and clear "contract" as the final results of negotiations. Conversely, the more networked Arab partners are more process oriented, making even more relevant the perception of procedural justice, and the final outcome is expected to be more a trust based, fluid, and somewhat ambiguous agreement that can therefore be supported by the different factions in their societies. Mishal and Morag conclude that these differences both in the negotiations cultures and in the expectations of the parties are a major obstacle to bilateral negotiations and make them more likely to fail since it is likely that at least one of the parties will find either the process or the outcome objectionable.

These difficulties have also been documented in actual negotiations between Israelis and Palestinians. Bar-Zion[14] was a member of the Israeli negotiating team during the Wye River–Oslo II process that was supposed to be a follow-up to the original Oslo agreements. He identified nine barriers that in his experience, as part of the Israeli team, contributed to the ultimate failure of the Oslo process:

1. high- vs. low-opening positions;

2. positional bargaining preventing value creation;

3. poor coordination within the Israeli delegation;

4. retraction of offers and its effect on trust building;

5. indirect information sharing vs. no information sharing;

6. lack of reciprocity;

7. linked negotiations and the impact of external events;

8. time pressure and last-minute concessions;

9. tactical use of language (p. 384).

Bar-Zion himself attributes most of these barriers to cultural differences, including "Israeli individualism versus Palestinian collectivism, Israeli egalitarian versus Palestinian hierarchical society, and Israeli low- versus Palestinian high-context communications" (p. 387). We have already explored many of these issues in more detail in this chapter, but Bar-Zion's perspective is particularly interesting because it refers to actual interactions in the context of real negotiations with the Palestinians. In one case, for instance, he relates how Palestinian negotiators felt insulted when the Israelis presented them with a detailed proposal to reduce car theft from Israel into the Palestinian territories (including lists of names and aerial photographs). The Palestinians were offended by the direct language of the document, which they found commanding and patronizing, and by the fact that the proposal seemed to put all of the responsibility (both for the thefts and for the solution) on the Palestinians. The incident gave the Palestinians a reason (an excuse, in Bar-Zion's perception) to become defensive and greatly damaged their mutual trust, which as we have discussed, for them is more important than the substance of the negotiations.

Interestingly, after Bar-Zion published his paper, Dajani,[15] who served as legal advisor for the Palestinian Authority on the same negotiating committee as Mr. Bar-Zion, presented his view, from a Palestinian perspective, of the barriers that led to the failure of the process. He begins, for instance, by pointing out that the power differential that exists between the sovereign Israeli government and the limited Palestinian Authority is already a barrier since, instead of being a dialogue of equals, it is already perceived by the Palestinians as inherently unfair. However, he also summarizes a number of other, more procedural, obstacles. He mentions for instance that Israelis were irritated by the more disorganized, fluid state of the Palestinian delegation (Palestinians have more tolerance for ambiguity and uncertainty) and in his view, many Israelis interpreted many of the problems arising from disorganization as "bad faith." Another example is Israel's refusal to accept neutral third party arbitration, instead of clear-cut and explicit rules and regulations in case of disputes, a major issue for the Palestinians who prefer more ambiguous regulations that can be agreed upon during mutual dialogue. Finally, the Palestinians were exasperated by what Dajani describes as "Israeli hypocrisy," citing for example issues in which they were demanding the Palestinian security services close the stolen car "chop shops" but at the same time being "commanded" not to meddle into internal Israeli police affairs. Or presenting them with aerial photographs of the West Bank, while at the same time preventing the Palestinians from acquiring and using their own photographs. These are examples of what Dajani says the Palestinians perceived as an Israeli "predilection for domination and control" (p. 406).

Precisely because of the complexities related to communication, organization, and perceptions of procedural and distributive justice, some researchers have suggested that alternative models of negotiations might perhaps be more effective. Cross and Rosenthal[16] did a simulation using Jewish, Arab Israeli, and American students of three different conflict resolution models to test their effectiveness. In the "distributive bargaining" model, which has characterized Israeli–Palestinian negotiations for decades, parties see the conflict as a zero-sum game, and the goal is to compete in the negotiation process to maximize gains at the expense of the rival. The outcome of the negotiation is an agreement that distributes the pie between the parties. Because of the competitive nature of this model, it is characteristic to use tactics such as withholding information, ambiguous goal setting, overt threats, bluffing, etc. The second model is "integrative bargaining," and it is characterized by searching for mutually profitable solutions. It is a win-win model that is based on the premise that both parties will profit from an end to the conflict, therefore increasing both sides' share of the pie. In order to reach an agreement, both parties have to make concessions and work cooperatively. In this model, information must be shared openly, goals defined clearly, and possible solutions explored honestly. Finally, "interactive problem solving" is a complex technique in which, instead of negotiation, both parties approach the conflict as a "problem" and interact in search of the best solutions. It is highly analytical, cooperative, and usually driven by an impartial third party mediator that can keep the sides from arguing and focus them on joint analysis. Because of the highly participatory and cooperative nature of this technique, it is much more likely to achieve positive solutions that are seen as procedurally and distributively fair by both sides. However, because of the same reasons, it is a very unlikely technique to be used by parties that deeply distrust and stereotype each other. As they expected, Cross and Rosenthal found that the simulation groups using the interactive problem solving approach had, without a doubt, the most positive change both in expectations related to the solving of the conflict and in attitudes toward the rival party. Interestingly, the groups using the integrative bargaining approach had the worst outcomes, while the distributive bargaining model was somewhere in the middle. Indeed, a couple of papers by Kelman[17,18] support the findings of Cross and Rosenthal. First, in a very perceptive political psychology essay, he analyzes the process and collapse of the Oslo peace agreement. He concludes that a solution to the conflict cannot lie today in a distributive bargaining model such as the one that led to the Oslo agreements. Instead, he advocates a more principled solution that has to be based on broad, basic principles, an approach more compatible with integrative bargaining or interactive problem solving. Kelman also recounts in an article in *American Psychologist*[19] the success in the field of a number of high-level workshops between Israeli and Palestinian personalities that he helped design and that followed the interactive problem solving model. In these workshops, which occurred in the early 1990s and were parallel to the Madrid conference and the Oslo Agreement, prominent Israeli and Palestinian figures met discreetly and unofficially to generate new ideas for solutions to the conflict. The participants were able not only to produce some positive insights but also to develop mutual understanding and relationships that were later transferred to the macro level of the political arena.

In summary, many difficulties exist in bilateral negotiations between Israelis and Palestinians. They have different communication styles, different perceptions of procedural justice and distributive justice, and different expectations and negotiating styles and are unlikely to find mediators that would be considered neutral by both sides. In addition, the political reality has led the parties every time they finally agree to begin dialogue to a distributive bargaining negotiation model, which is competitive and antagonistic, and is therefore the least likely to lead to a mutually agreed solution. Finally, all of these obstacles are on top of the existing stereotypes and prejudices, which themselves make it difficult to reach an agreement. However, successful dialogue is not impossible. It must begin by understanding and acknowledging all of these differences and then adopting a more flexible structure of negotiations in which both cultures can be accommodated. Mishal and Morag suggest a dialogue model that they call "perceptual pluralism" which in essence proposes that, instead of a tit-for-tat agreement in which each side makes equivalent, symmetrical concessions in each issue in dispute, the two sides must be willing to accept asymmetric arrangements (e.g., Palestinians willing to limit troops, while not demanding the same from Israelis, or Israelis limiting access to Palestinian markets, while giving full access to their own) but provide very little empirical evidence that such an arrangement would work. Similarly, Cross and Rosenthal,[20] based on the research they conducted with alternative dialogue models, which we have discussed above, suggest that an interactive problem-solving approach could be a lot more beneficial.

What is certain is that before any dialogue can be successful, both parties have to be a lot more open to understand the other party and their cultural differences and have to be willing to set aside their stereotypes and prejudices. This is a process that is a lot more complex and takes a lot longer than just political negotiations. How can we get there? How can we set the foundations that can lead to a successful resolution of the conflict?

The Search for a Solution

Economic Interaction

A solution to the Israeli–Palestinian conflict depends on a complex, multifaceted process in which interactions need to occur at a variety of levels, including the economic level. And, of course, one of the big recompenses of peace is that it enables a normalization of life and an improvement in life quality and standards of living. In the view of many analysts, this should be a major motivator to help bring about dialogue and ultimately peace and reconciliation. For example, a study that looked at the effects of economics on the attitudes of Israelis and Palestinians was carried out by Nachtwey and Tessler[21] in 2002. They analyzed original surveys given to over 1,100 Israelis in 1996 and to 1,200 Palestinians in 1999 and then follow-up surveys completed by about 1,300 Palestinians and over 500 Israelis in 2001. Although the three sets of surveys were somewhat different, all of the included questions were about support for a negotiated solution and recognition of the other party's rights [e.g., "After reaching a peace agreement between the Palestinian people and Israel and the establishment of a Palestinian state that is recognized by Israel, do you support or oppose the process of reconciliation between the state of Palestine and the state of Israel?" (p. 272)] and about both the general social economic impact and the personal economic situation of the participants [e.g., "If a peace agreement is reached, what will its economic impact be for the Palestinian people in general?" and "Rate your own family's standard of living" (p. 273)]. Nachtwey and Tessler found that indeed, Palestinians and Israelis who think that peace will improve their national economies are more likely to support dialogue and make territorial concessions than those who do not believe an agreement will improve the economy. In another paper, Friedman[22] proposes that engaging the sides in mutual economic enterprises and using economic incentives can help the enemies soften their views toward conflict. Friedman gave questionnaires to over nine hundred participants and then did a statistical analysis to determine if changes in the economic situation and expectations of the Palestinians had an effect on their views regarding peace and violence toward the Israelis. He not only collected some factual information such as income and educational levels but also asked questions about expectations such as economic integration and the impact of any future peace agreement on the economy. In addition, he asked the participants' opinions regarding diplomacy and attacks against Israel. Friedman found that although some of the aspects of a "peace dividend" could help motivate Palestinians to move from violence toward diplomacy, others do not. He found, for example, that the expectation of general economic improvements and economic integration between Palestinians and Israelis can have an impact on the participants' views regarding diplomacy. On the other hand, he also discovered that the economic impact of the Intifada does not affect their views. Issues like personal economic incentives play a role among people who care a lot about the economy, but not for the general sample. In summary, Friedman found that the expectations of improved economic conditions has a moderate effect on the Palestinians' view of violence and diplomacy, but it is not a determinant factor.

It is very important, therefore, to point out that, as Mazen suggests in a 1998 article,[23] even though the potential for a huge "peace dividend" and economic impact exists in a peace agreement, economic ties are not possible without a change in attitudes among the general population. Mazen relates a case study of a successful Jordanian-Palestinian entrepreneur who began a very promising joint venture with Israelis after the 1994 Israel–Jordan peace treaty, only to be forced to severe his ties because of boycotts of his company and even personal threats by the local population. In conclusion, then, even though the expectation of economic gains and an improvement in standards of living are potentially a positive motivator that can help the dialogue and reconciliation process, it is clear that before that level can be achieved, there has to be a comprehensive change at a more basic social and cultural level that will allow people to enjoy or even just consider the economic benefits of peace.

Group Encounters

One of the methods that has been widely used to foster attitude change and reconciliation in intergroup conflict has been, of course, the use of joint encounters between members of the enemy factions. These encounters have occurred both at the grass roots level and at the political level. We must ask, however, under what circumstances, if at all, are these encounters helpful. Are they being effective to reduce prejudice and other psychological barriers and increase understanding between the two peoples? In the past few decades, theoretical support for the effectiveness of these types of workshops has been mostly based on the original "contact hypothesis" proposed by renowned psychologist Allport.[24] He suggested that prejudice could be reduced by merely increasing the contact between two mutually prejudiced groups. Zajonc[25] developed a more elaborate model based on the contact hypothesis, which he called the "mere exposure effect." According to Zajonc, the mere exposure to other people can be enough to help us reduce interpersonal barriers. His research showed that, for example, the more times a person was exposed to a stranger, the more he or she liked him or her, even though there was no other interaction between the subject and the stranger.

Social psychologist Kelman[26] reviewed research like this and other research in social psychology to try to determine if, and in what conditions, exposure and contact between Palestinians and Israelis could help with reconciliation. He suggests that, based on a lengthy body of research, in order for these types of encounters to be effective it is not enough to have "dialogue encounters," but that a common goal has to be sought in order to get the participants to focus on solutions instead of taking the opportunity for recrimination. He recommended a format of problem-solving workshops, much like the ones carried out by Israeli and Palestinian political leaders before the signing of the Oslo accords in 1993. Tal-Or and her colleagues[27] also did an analysis of the conditions necessary for effective intergroup encounters between Israelis and Palestinians. Their extensive review of the theories and current research yielded the following conditions as necessary for successful intergroup encounters:

Social conditions

1. Close contact, which should be prolonged and frequent.
2. Cooperation, shared goals instead of competition.
3. Equal status, even if in the outside world the groups have a superior and inferior status.

Cognitive conditions

1. Decategorization: The meeting has to be set up in a way that encourages contact between *individuals* and not groups, to minimize cognitive categorization.

2. Recategorization: Building a common identity through identification with a group *in common* between the participants.
3. Reduce stereotyping: Focus on the individual, for example, emphasize the individual characteristics that mismatch the group stereotypes.

Even though there have been a large number of programs to promote intergroup encounters between Israelis and Palestinians, these conditions have rarely been applied to most of them. Suleiman,[28] from the University of Haifa, observed that most of these encounters are ineffective because

a flawed characterization of the goals and a faulty understanding of the processes that took place in the group and of what is necessary for generating the desired changes, have all led to irrelevant considerations in determining the nature of the group and the facilitation style (p. 324).

And psychologists Ben-Ari and Amir[29] note that "the quality and scientific merit of this work are far from satisfactory. Many programs for 'change' have been designed, but in most of them the goals have not been well defined, and their theoretical foundations are not always clear" (p. 50). Suleiman proposes a model based on the social identification theory, which is consistent with the recommendations put forward by Tal-Or and her colleagues. In essence, he suggests to manage interpersonal communication processes so they will "cultivate" intergroup dialogue and that participants be provided with relevant background information, including research on group power differential.

Probably the researcher who has studied intergroup encounters between Israelis and Palestinians most in depth is Maoz,[30] from the Hebrew University of Jerusalem. In a large series of studies, Maoz has identified a number of characteristics that facilitate successful dialogue between the parties and also factors that impede positive outcomes. For example, in one study[31] Maoz and others analyze the detailed narrative of an unsuccessful encounter between a group of graduate students, seven Palestinian Israelis (five men and two women) and seven Jewish Israelis (three men and four women). Maoz and her colleagues describe repeated attempts by a couple of the Jewish participants to monopolize the discourse, and at the same time, delegitimize and even attempt to silence the Palestinian narrative, reflecting the reality of power differential in the society at large. Maoz sees this behavior as a repeating pattern in Israeli society and explains that "Israeli Jews' fear that if they begin listening to Palestinians, they (Israeli Jews) will not be able to continue being who they are" (p. 1079). In another, more comprehensive study, Maoz[32] analyzes forty-seven encounter programs between Israeli Jews and Palestinians that took place between 1999 and 2000. She identified "symmetry," which refers to the degree to which participants of both groups take part equally in the interaction throughout the encounter dialogue, as the core factor that can make these dialogues successful. She did find that in about 89% of these programs, there was very good symmetry between the Jewish and the Palestinian participants. However, only in 45% was there symmetry among the facilitators, who typically include a Jewish and Palestinian dyad. In another 45% of the cases, there was dominance by the Jewish facilitator, again reflecting the power differential in the larger social groups. This symmetry is critical, because, as Maoz observes, programs she studied in the 1980s,[33] which reflected a much more asymmetrical relationship, were in some cases even counterproductive because they "led to or enhanced, in many cases, negative intergroup intrinsic attributions and stereotyping on the part of the participants and staff involved in these encounters" (p. 450). Overall, from her studies, we can conclude that the facilitator's role to equalize power and mediate effectively is extremely important. When these conditions are met, as Maoz found in another study,[34] intergroup encounters can be really successful at bringing about changes in attitudes and implicit stereotypes, especially among the more hawkish participants.

Other researchers have also found that group encounters can lead to positive outcomes if they are symmetrical, structured, and well facilitated. In a 2004 study, Bargal[35] found that traditional conflict management techniques were no longer being successful because of the recent escalation in violence after the eruption of the 2000 Intifada, which has generated "cognitive distortions, anger, hostility, fear, grief, victimization, and humiliation" (p. 597). Instead, he proposes a more successful approach that he calls "reconciliation-transformation" workshops, which are structured more as a therapeutic group environment and require much more controlled facilitation. A similar approach is proposed by Sagy, Steinberg, and Faheraladin,[36] who present two models that are also reminiscent of therapeutic group techniques and are focused on identity and interpersonal dimensions.

Finally, Mollov and Lavie[37] also studied a group of Israeli Jewish and Palestinian university students engaged in intergroup dialogue. Based on the results from their study, they suggest that encounters based on common religious and faith issues can be successful, because Jewish and Muslim participants can find many similarities and commonalities between their respective faiths, and that can help reduce stereotypes and bridge the in-group-out-group gap.

Social and Cultural Events

Israelis and Palestinians share very little in terms of common opportunities to participate in social and cultural activities. Even within Israel, Israeli Jews and Israeli Arabs very seldom get together to celebrate or commemorate common events. Israeli national holidays, such as Yom Haatzmaut (Independence Day) and Yom Hazikaron (Memorial Day), are in fact days of national tragedy and mourning among Palestinians, when they remember their Nakba (Tragedy). Religious holidays are completely different since Jews, Muslims, and Christians do not share any festivals in common. Even cultural activities such as fairs and concerts are largely segregated, even when the performers are international artists who are well known on both sides of the green line. On the other hand, there have been some attempts to bring Israelis, Israeli Arabs, and Palestinians together. For instance, the Shimon Peres' Center for Peace sponsored a joint Israeli–Palestinian soccer team, nicknamed the Peace Team, which played a number of international exhibitions. On some occasions, Israeli and Palestinian artists have collaborated in some projects, like the Israeli singer David Broza and the Palestinian Wissam Murad who cowrote and performed the same song in Hebrew and Arabic versions, "My Heart," in 2005. The fact that some, even if few, projects are carried out shows that many of the barriers to joint cultural and social programs are artificial ones, and a few researchers have looked at the possibility of using cultural and social activities to attempt to bring the sides together.

For example, Bekerman[38] analyzed the effects of having joint commemoration and celebration ceremonies in two joint Jewish–Palestinian bilingual elementary schools, one in Jerusalem and the other in the Galilee, which opened in 1997 during the lull in violence that came after the Oslo accords. He focused on the role of two ceremonies: the first was a more neutral Hanukkah–Eid-al-Fitr–Christmas multicultural celebration, which attempted to emphasize the commonalities of the festivals. Hanukkah, the festival of lights, is the Jewish celebration of the ancient victory of the Israelites over the Hellenistic Seleucid empire and typically falls in December every year. Eid-al-Fitr is the celebration that marks the end of the holy month of Ramadan, when Muslims fast during the daytime for a full month. While it is celebrated at a different time every year because the lunar year that marks the Muslim calendar is slightly shorter than the solar year, in 2000 and 2001 the festival was also celebrated around December. And finally, Christmas is the Christian celebration of the birth of Jesus about 2,000 years ago. The second event was a more complex ceremony carried out during the Israeli Memorial Day, and in order to become a cross-cultural event, was redesigned to include the Palestinian narrative of the Nakba (Disaster), and become a true commemoration of those who had to pay the ultimate price due to the binational conflict. The results of Bekerman's study are somewhat encouraging, but ultimately inconclusive. While in the first year of the study it was clear that students, teachers, and parents were very satisfied with the results and both events seemed to clearly help the students understand the perspective of the "other side," the second year was problematic. The study was carried out in 2000–01, and the second year of the study occurred after the Al-Aqsa Intifada had started. The Hanukkah–Eid-al-Fitr–Christmas ceremony was colder, and the Memorial day was outright problematic, to the point that some parents expressed dissatisfaction and outrage. Nevertheless, Bekerman suggests that under the right circumstances, joint celebrations and commemoration have a great potential to bring the two peoples closer.

Certainly, we cannot talk about joint cultural issues in the twenty-first century without including the role of television. Israeli television, since its inception, has carried a daily Arabic news program and some minimal Arabic programming among its largely Hebrew lineup. Many Palestinian broadcasters also feature Hebrew language Web sites and news programs. However, there are very few attempts to organize joint programming. One of the very few exceptions is a cooperative Israeli and Palestinian edition of Jim Henson's *Sesame Street,* known as *Rechov Sumsum/Shara'a Simsim* in Hebrew and in Arabic, respectively. This bilingual series, coproduced by Israel Educational Television in association with Al-Quds University's Institute for Modern Media and the New York based Children's Television Workshop, began airing in Israel and the Palestinian territories in 1998. Cole and her colleagues[39] studied the effects of watching the series in Israeli and Palestinian preschool-aged children. They measured the attitudes of the children before the beginning of the broadcast and then again after four months of watching the program. Once again, the results of Cole's study are mixed. On the one hand, the Israeli and Israeli Palestinian children showed much more positive attitudes and attributions regarding the Palestinians. However, the Palestinian children showed no improvement. Conversely, Israeli children had no change after the program regarding pro-social judgments (being nice to others), while Palestinian children improved in their pro-social reasoning. Cole and her colleagues conclude with a cautiously positive note, pointing out that there were some positive effects in all the groups of children and that television programs that emphasize coexistence can play an important role in bringing about reconciliation.

Overall, it is clear that cooperative social and cultural projects have a very minimal downside. Even though most of the results from empirical studies are mixed or inconclusive, there are always some positive aspects to them. Besides, we cannot take these events in isolation from their larger context. The projects at the bilingual schools, for example, seemed to go in a very positive direction before the eruption of the Al-Aqsa Intifada. But it would be naïve to believe that ceremonies and celebration will have a more powerful effect on young people than the events on the streets. In my opinion, the best hope for changing attitudes and reducing stereotypes and prejudice lies not in isolated events, sporadic workshops, or impersonal television programming, but in the only institutions that have an intensive day-to-day contact with the young generations. The only way to bring about lasting change toward real reconciliation lies in education.

Education

Education, of course, has always been at the forefront of any attempts to bring about reconciliation and coexistence between Israelis and Palestinians. According to the Abraham Fund,[40] a nonprofit organization dedicated to Israeli–Arab coexistence, over 300 projects, involving more than 150,000 people, have been developed and carried out in the past few decades, sometimes successfully, sometimes with mixed results, but always with the heavy feeling that they have been efforts against the huge flow of political events, amounting, at best, to a small drop in a sea of hatred and hostility. However, in psychology, we know that perception is usually not the same thing as reality, and therefore for this book I am compelled to ask: Have existing educational projects *been* successful at bringing about attitude change and rapprochement? What are the characteristics of programs that work? And finally, can we do it better?

Once again, unfortunately, we have very little data regarding programs on the Palestinian side of the conflict, and therefore in order to answer these questions, I am forced to rely mainly on data from Israeli researchers.

Some of the promising types of programs that have reported success in education for coexistence are the handful of joint bilingual and bicultural Jewish-Arab schools in Israel. And one of the most successful and renowned of these programs is the Neve Shalom/Wahat Al-Salam Jewish-Arab School for Peace. Neve Shalom/Wahat Al-Salam (Oasis of Peace in Hebrew and Arabic) is a small village of about two hundred people, located near Jerusalem, and founded jointly by Israeli Jewish and Palestinian citizens in 1972, who wanted to set an example of peace and coexistence. The village has two educational institutions, a bicultural/bilingual preschool to eighth-grade school for children from the village and surrounding communities and the School for Peace, which conducts both intensive seminars and extensive, residential three- to six-month-long programs for high school students. Feuerverger[41] conducted a number of in-depth qualitative evaluations of both programs. She found that in both cases the programs were quite successful at creating a positive coexistence atmosphere and positive attitudes of respect and tolerance of cultural and national identities. In addition, her research suggests that there are a number of elements that make the Neve Shalom/Wahat Al-Salam educational projects successful. First, there is total symmetry regarding the importance of language and culture. For example, Hebrew and Arabic are taught and used as a teaching language in the exact same proportion, and national narratives are equally validated in the curriculum. Second, a cooperative decision making process in which students and teachers have a voice and their opinions are respected. This process promotes a message of diversity, respect, and democracy, in which the teachers, instead of being seen as authoritative figures, are seen as facilitators whose role is to promote the personal growth and development of the child, and the children are seen as individual, capable persons with the ability to take responsibility over the decisions made in school. Third, Feuerverger suggests that the focus of the schools on the moral development of the children through dialogue and personal narrative plays a crucial role in its success. The educational projects, instead of shying away from controversial, morally complex topics, encourage their exploration and difficult dialogue. These interactions not only help children develop into morally complex, tolerant individuals but also help them understand and empathize with the issues facing the "other" nation.

Other successful bilingual and bicultural school projects have been reported by Glazier[42] and by the Hand in Hand Center for Jewish-Arab Education,[43] which operates three elementary schools: one in the Galilee, one in Jerusalem, and one in the Wadi Ara region of northern Israel. All of these schools have reported great success in terms of developing multicultural awareness and fostering coexistence, and Glazier concludes that they have a significant impact on the attitudes and openness to diversity of the students. The main obstacle to this type of reconciliation effort, however, is that there are only half a dozen schools of this type in Israel. There is strong opposition both among Israeli Jews and among Israeli Arabs to desegregate the Israeli education system because each group wants to zealously preserve their own cultural and historic heritage. Some authors, for example, Dwairy,[44] actually suggest that Israeli policies of "modernization" of education are not sensitive to the culture of Israeli Arab citizens and that as a matter of fact, what is needed in order to foster good will and understanding is for the Israelis to develop a more culturally sensitive educational policy that respects Arab values and norms and will allow Arabs to develop their own educational programs without Israeli interference.

A different type of approach that seems to be more acceptable to Israelis, and therefore is more widespread, is to focus on developing multicultural education, stereotype reduction, and tolerance-based programs within the existing educational framework. One such program is proposed by Helena Desiviliya from the Emek Yezreel College. She suggests that an educational model that is based on a psychological intervention known as MACBE can help reduce fear, hate, and resentment and therefore set forward the conditions for rapprochement. The model is named after the basic modalities of human experience that are normally the areas which deteriorate during interpersonal conflict: Motivation, Affect, Cognition, Behavior, and Environment. Desiviliya further suggests that all of these modalities must be treated systemically, in tandem, in order to reduce conflict, to avoid the dynamic of circularity, in which if one of the modalities is not treated, it will reinitiate the cycle of conflict. She therefore put together a continuous educational program, designed to train educators and facilitators, that includes components directed simultaneously at each of the five modalities mentioned above. She conducted a sample program in northern Israel in 1999, in which the participants were local Israeli Arab and Jewish school principals and counselors. Desiviliya reported that the intervention program was successful at giving the educators the tools they need to better educate toward coexistence and reduce conflict and its effects. She concludes that even though it would be very difficult to implement the MACBE model in its full, systemic form, even partial application of the program can "contribute to peaceful coexistence of adversary groups" (p. 353) and improve relationships between Arabs and Jews in Israel.

Another strategy to reduce stereotypes among Israeli children was proposed by Slone, Tarrasch, and Hallis.[45] They carried out two different school-based intervention programs, one based on textual content, the other one on audiovisual content, to about 200 Israeli Jewish fifth grade children. In the textual content program, children would read stories related to contact between Israeli Jews and Arabs and then have an open discussion about cognitive and emotional issues related to the story. The audiovisual program was similar, except instead of a written story, the facilitators would use excerpts from films. The meetings occurred once a week, and the intervention programs lasted for six weeks. Slone and her colleagues found that there was a significant reduction in the levels of stereotypes the children had regarding Arabs in both programs, and given the relatively short and simple nature of these interventions, they suggest that this could be easily implemented in regular classrooms as part of the normal curriculum. These results are encouraging since these interventions are simple, short, and easily implemented. However, Slone and her colleagues do not do any follow-up on the participants, so we cannot know if their results are just a short-term change in attitudes or a real long-lasting effect on their stereotypical beliefs.

A much more comprehensive and long-term approach is suggested by Hertz-Lazarowitz,[46] who carried out a five-year action research project in the northern Israeli city of Acre. The city of Acre is a mixed Jewish-Arab city that has had relatively good relationships between its two national groups. Recently, it was singled out as a model of cooperative problem solving, as both Jewish and Arab citizens were able to maintain a pacific coexistence while being bombarded by missiles in the Israel-Hezbollah war in Lebanon.[47] In spite of the relatively good relationships between the Jewish and the Arab inhabitants, Acre also suffers from many of the stereotypes, prejudice, and discrimination against Israeli Arabs that is embedded in much of the Israeli establishment. In this background, the local and national governments started a systemic five-year program in 1995 "to empower the educational community to work together to improve the academic and social outcomes of all the students in Acre"

(p. 358). The program, known as CILC (Cooperation, Investigation of problems, Literacy, and Community), was a complex, multilayered, and multiarea project, whose main component was the creation of joint Arab-Jewish task forces in different areas to analyze and propose parallel initiatives to improve equality and coexistence. There were parental task forces, administrator task forces, teacher task forces, and students' encounters. The work in common was based on the "spirit of holism, democracy, coexistence, and multiculturalism" (p. 359), and the common goal was "to increase and equalize educational achievements of Arab and Jewish students in Acre" (p. 360). At the end of the project in 1999, Hertz-Lazarowitz reported that it was a total success that led to more educational equality, better overall outcomes, and a sense of empowerment by the community that even led to political change to a Jewish-Arab coalition in city government. Nevertheless, a few months later, the Al-Aqsa Intifada erupted, and thirteen Israeli Arabs were killed during a demonstration. Those events strained to a degree the positive relations that had developed between Jews and Arabs, and at the time of a follow-up in early 2001, Hertz-Lazarowitz was not entirely optimistic about the future of relationships in the city. Although the spirit of cooperation and community that existed in 1999 might have eroded, the fact that during the very controversial Israel-Hezbollah war relationships remained positive might be a testament to the success of the original program.

As we can see, even with the best and most sophisticated programs, it is hard to say unequivocally that education toward peace can be effective as long as we have an ongoing, protracted conflict going on. The unavoidable truth is that no matter what we do in an educational setting, the reality in the field is going to be much stronger and more influential in peoples' views and attitudes. So, can peace education really make a difference under these circumstances, or are we talking about an exercise in futility? Salomon, from the Center for Research on Peace Education at the University of Haifa, conducted an analysis of the research regarding peace education programs in Israel to determine if, and under what circumstances, they can be effective.[48] This was no easy task, since as Salomon indicates, there is a surprising lack of evaluation research regarding peace education programs, in spite of the fact that these programs are numerous and worldwide. First, Salomon points out a number of hurdles that any successful program must overcome: it has to challenge the collectively held beliefs about "us" and about "them"; it has to deal with the built-in inequalities between Israelis and Palestinians; it has to provide mechanisms to control excessive emotionality; and it has to acknowledge and deal with a context of animosity, fear, and belligerence.

Then, Salomon analyzes a number of studies that have looked at peace education programs among Israelis and Palestinians. For example, in one program, both Israeli and Palestinian high school students studied about a foreign conflict (Northern Ireland) and were left to transfer knowledge and reach conclusions about their own conflict on their own (although the Palestinian participants dropped out of the evaluation study because of the beginning of the Intifada). In another study with over 800 high school students who participated in a year-long program, the focus was to study "peace" rather than the conflict directly, with numerous meetings between Palestinians and Israelis. Overall, Salomon's results were cautiously encouraging, indicating increased empathy, more positive attitudes toward peace and conflict resolution, lower stereotypes, and the ability to see the other side's point of view.

From the research we have discussed thus far, we must conclude that even though education does seem to have a positive effect regarding stereotypes, beliefs, and attitudes toward peace, it is definitely not a silver bullet. Most of the educational projects evaluated tend to have qualified positive results. Herein, however, lies a catch. Most of the educational programs reviewed tend to be focused on a traditional educational paradigm. For the most part, they are carried out among regular students, and their focus tends to be on dealing with issues directly related to the conflict (even in the cases in which a peripheral route is taken, like the Northern Ireland focused program). Perhaps, the solution lies not with the implementation of direct programs in traditional settings, but rather, on something a lot more basic. Perhaps we need to think outside the box and have a paradigm shift if we want to be successful in educating a new generation of people committed to peace and coexistence.

Alternative Pedagogies: Can It Be the Answer?

In his foreword to the classical work by Paulo Freire, *Pedagogy of the Oppressed*,[49] Richard Shaull writes that:

Education either functions as an instrument which is used to facilitate the integration of the younger generation into the logic of the present system and bring about conformity to it, or it becomes "the practice of freedom", the means by which men and women deal critically and creatively with reality and discover how to participate in the transformation of their world (p. 16).

In Shaull's terms, then, if the logic of the present system is one of conflict and hatred, the answer to the alternatives he presents is clearly transformation and not conformity. Is it possible that the answer to a long-lasting resolution to the conflict lies not with all the direct peace education and conflict resolution programs, but rather with what Shaull calls "the practice of freedom?" If, as we discussed from the beginning of this book, the psychological root of these conflicts is the narrow beliefs which lead to stereotypes and prejudice, to hate and misconceptions, then, logically, the solution could be found in critical thinking, cooperation, creativity, and an education whose methodology is consistent with a message of equality and democracy. Children who are educated on critical thinking instead of conformity, on cooperation instead of competition, are a lot more likely to be able to see the conflict as a solvable problem and to have the ability to take the other's perspective and empathize with them. Is there any evidence, then, that education that is focused on the development of the child as a critical thinking person can really lead to a more empathic, compassionate individual and therefore lead to lower stereotypes and greater tolerance?

There are a number of pedagogical philosophies that emphasize critical thinking, cooperation and mastery over narrow problem solving, individual work, and performance. Some of them like critical pedagogy, democratic education, and the jigsaw classroom have been separately researched in relation to areas like tolerance, diversity, empathy, and compassion. But in order to analyze all of these alternative philosophies together, the most useful model is the learner-centered educational theory. The learner-centered model and its principles were first compiled by a special Presidential Task Force of the American Psychological Association, which looked at what contemporary research on learning, development, and cognition could tell about the best way to educate children and adults. The model was further developed throughout the 1990s by McCombs and Whisler.[50] The model can be summarized, in practice, by a number of specific classroom practices for the students (p. 10):

- Choice regarding their own projects and graded assignments, being able to select areas that are personally relevant.
- Individual pace—flexibility of time.

- Demonstrate their knowledge in unique ways—mastery orientation, feedback instead of grades, encourages risk taking instead of conformity.
- Learning is active. The students are engaged and participate in individual and group learning activities.
- Increasing responsibility for the learning process; for example, attendance is up to them.
- Refine their understanding by using critical thinking skills instead of searching for narrow, correct/incorrect type answers.

Indeed, Shapiro,[51] from the University of North Carolina at Greensboro, for example, suggests precisely that the use of critical pedagogy to address political conflict, since it fosters a positive view of nonviolence to solve conflicts, encourages critical thinking and questioning authority and promotes multiculturalism and openness to diversity, and is based on basic principles of democracy and compassion.

Although there have not been any studies that directly investigate if education that conforms with the learner-centered model has had a positive effect regarding the Israeli–Palestinian conflict, we do have some indirect evidence that suggests that this would be a promising approach if what we want to achieve is a long-term, lasting solution. First, the Neve Shalom/Wahat Al-Salam schools, which are arguably the most successful educational coexistence projects in the region, actually follow a model that conforms to the learner-centered parameters. Both the elementary school and the high school "School for Peace" programs are based on cooperative learning, active pedagogies, and shared decision making between teachers and students.

Additional evidence supporting this idea comes from renowned social psychologist Elliot Aronson, who developed the jigsaw classroom technique and has done a considerable body of research regarding its effects.[52] In this technique, students work on specific projects in small groups. They make decisions about how to divide the work and then work individually doing research. Then they get back together and work cooperatively to assemble their projects. Each student has a piece of the jigsaw puzzle, and each is essential. The research shows that students who learn in this type of classroom have amazingly positive effects on reduced prejudice and violence and increased empathy, tolerance, compassion, and critical thinking. Other research has provided even further evidence that learner-centered approaches can lead to a newer generation of people better skilled to achieve peace and reconciliation. For example,

Kenan[53] analyzes a learner-centered educational project adopted by New York City after the 9/11 terrorist attacks called *(Re)embracing Diversity in New York City Public Schools: Educational Outreach for Muslim Sensitivity,* whose aim was to foster tolerance and diversity appreciation. Kenan concludes that the program is an effective tool to "foster problem solving, critical reflection, and collaborative learning" (p. 172). Finally, a recent study[54] that I have just completed with my assistant, Joanna Garr, in which we compared students in six learner-centered schools and six control schools in different states in the United States, found that the students in the learner-centered schools scored significantly higher in diversity appreciation, tolerance, and initiative than their peers in regular schools.

One more reason why exploring learner-centered education as an avenue to promote peace and reconciliation is worthwhile is because Israel in particular has a strong tradition of embracing alternative pedagogies, albeit usually in small, experimental scales. A number of experimental schools have been opened in Israel since its independence, and the 100-year-old kibbutz movement educational system has always been progressive and learner-centered. Moreover, today, Israel is the leader country in the world in the democratic education movement, founded by Yaacov Hecht about a quarter century ago. There are more than twenty-five democratic schools in Israel, and all of them promote the idea of participatory decision making, critical thinking, choice for students, and active education, which are the staple of the learner-centered methodologies. Although I cannot answer conclusively, with the available evidence, if learner-centered education can be the solution for a new generation of Israeli and Palestinian children to be able to finally move toward peace, I can strongly argue that it is a possibility that is worth exploring.

Chapter Conclusion

There is no easy road to peace. Specially, because in order to achieve it, Israelis and Palestinians would need to begin by shedding many stereotypes, prejudice, and misconceptions. Furthermore, the hatred, the pain, the personal feeling of being hurt, and the desire for vengeance take this conflict beyond a political realm and make it a personal one for countless Palestinians and Israelis who feel personally aggrieved by the actions of their enemies. However, it is clear from the review of the research that a lot more could be done to bring us closer to it than what is currently done. We need to see a change in the negotiation paradigm, move away from a distributive bargaining model that is competitive and leaves both parties with a sense of "conceding" and into a more interactive problem-solving one with its win-win implications. We need to foster and promote more dialogue and encounters, and more economic ventures and business ties, not stifle them. We need to learn more about the "other" culture to build empathy and understanding and to move away from the stereotypes and the prejudice. But most important, we need to educate a new generation of children who are more open, tolerant, and empathic; who are more compassionate and know that conflict is resolved through dialogue and not violence; and who are critical thinkers and have the ability to understand and challenge preconceived notions. Because even if we do achieve a negotiated peace in our generation, the only guarantee for a genuine long-lasting peace between Palestinians and Israelis is a change in the mind-set of the people, and not their signatures on a treaty.

Notes

1. Chris McGreal at Kibbutz Metzer, "Kibbutz Unshaken in Pursuit of Utopia; Murders Only Increase Community's Belief in Coexistence With Arabs," *Guardian,* November 16, 2002.

2. Ellen Kussman Feghali, "Arab Cultural Communication Patterns," *International Journal of Intercultural Relations* 21, no. 3 (1997): 345–78.

3. E. T. Hall, *The Silent Language* (New York: Doubleday, 1959); E. T. Hall, *The Hidden Dimension* (New York: Doubleday, 1966).

4. R. Cohen, "Problems of Intercultural Communication in Egyptian-American Diplomatic Relations," *International Journal of Intercultural Relations* 11 (1987): 29–47; R. Cohen, *Culture and Conflict in Egyptian-Israeli Relations: A Dialogue of the Deaf* (Indianapolis, IN: Indiana University Press, 1990a); R. Cohen, "Deadlock: Israel and Egypt Negotiate," in *Communicating for Peace,* ed. F. Korzenny and S. Ting-Toomey (Newbury Park, CA: Sage, 1990b), 136–153.

5. T. Katriel, *Talking Straight: Dugri Speech in Israeli Sabra Culture* (Cambridge, MA: Cambridge University Press, 1986); Y. Griefat and T. Katriel , "Life Demands *Musayra:* Communication and Culture Among Arabs in Israel," in *Language, Communication and Culture,* ed. S. Ting-Toomey and F. Korzenny (Newbury Park, CA: Sage, 1989), 121–38.

6. Donald G. Ellis and Ifat Maoz, "Cross-Cultural Argument Interactions Between Israeli-Jews and Palestinians," *Journal of Applied Communication Research* 30, no. 3 (2002): 181–94.

7. Valerie Manusov and Tema Milstein, "Interpreting Nonverbal Behavior: Representation and Transformation Frames in Israeli and Palestinian Media Coverage of the 1993 Rabin–Arafat Handshake," *Western Journal of Communication* 69, no. 3 (2005): 183–201.

8. William A. Donohue, "The Language of Equivocation," in "Managing Equivocality and Relational Paradox in the Oslo Peace Negotiations," *Journal of Language and Social Psychology* 17, no. 1 (1998): 72–96.

9. E. Allan Lind and Tom R. Tyler, *The Social Psychology of Procedural Justice* (New York: Plenum Press, 1988).

10. Karen A. Hegtvedt and Caitlin Killian, "Fairness and Emotions: Reactions to the Process and Outcomes of Negotiations," *Social Forces* 78, no. 1 (1999): 269–303.

11. A. Paul Hare, Bassam Al Ashhab, and Gideon M. Kressel, "Perceptions of the Ideal Mediator: An Israeli-Palestinian Example," *Psychological Reports* 93, no. 3 (2003): 771–75.

12. Philip A. Schrodt and Deborah J. Gerner, "An Event Data Analysis of Third-Party Mediation in the Middle East and Balkans," *Journal of Conflict Resolution* 48, no. 3 (2004): 310–330.

13. Shaul Mishal and Nadav Morag, "Political Expectations and Cultural Perceptions in the Arab-Israeli Peace Negotiations," *Political Psychology* 23, no. 2 (2002): 325–53.

14. Bari Bar-Zion, "Understanding Barriers to Peace: Reflecting on Israeli-Palestinian Economic Negotiations," *Negotiation Journal* 20, no. 3 (2004): 383–400.

15. Omar M. Dajani, "Understanding Barriers to Peace: A Palestinian Response," *Negotiation Journal* 20, no. 3 (2004): 401–8.

16. Susan Cross and Robert Rosenthal, "Prejudice and Intergroup Relations: Papers in Honor of Gordon W. Allport's Centennial," in "Three Models of Conflict Resolution: Effects on Intergroup Expectancies and Attitudes," *Journal of Social Issues* 55, no. 3 (1999): 561–80.

17. Herbert C. Kelman, "Building a Sustainable Peace: The Limits of Pragmatism in the Israeli-Palestinian Negotiations," *Peace & Conflict: Journal of Peace Psychology* 5, no. 2 (1999): 101–15.

18. Herbert C. Kelman, "Group Processes in the Resolution of International Conflicts: Experiences From the Israeli-Palestinian Case," *American Psychologist* 52, no. 3 (1997): 212–20.

19. Ibid.

20. Cross and Rosenthal, "Prejudice and Intergroup Relations."

21. Jodi Nachtwey and Mark Tessler, "The Political Economy of Attitudes Toward Peace Among Palestinians and Israelis," *Journal of Conflict Resolution* 46, no. 2 (2002): 260–85.

22. Gil Friedman, "Commercial Pacifism and Protracted Conflict: Models From the Palestinian-Israeli Case," *Journal of Conflict Resolution* 49, no. 3 (2005): 360–82.

23. Abdelmagid M. Mazen, "When Settlement and Resolution are in Conflict: Searching for a Mideast Peace Dividend," *Negotiation Journal* 14, no. 4 (1998): 357–67.

24. G. W. Allport, *The Nature of Prejudice* (Reading, MA: Addison-Wesley, 1954).

25. Robert B. Zajonc, "Attitudinal Effects of Mere Exposure," *Journal of Personality and Social Psychology* 9, Suppl. (June 1968): 1–27.

26. Herbert C. Kelman, "Political Psychology," in "Social-Psychological Contributions to Peacemaking and Peacebuilding in the Middle East," *Applied Psychology: An International Review* 47, no. 1 (1998): 5–28.

27. Nurit Tal-Or, David Boninger, and Faith Gleicher, "Understanding the Conditions and Processes Necessary for Intergroup Contact to Reduce Prejudice," in *Peace Education: The Concept, Principles, and Practices Around the World,* ed. Gavriel Salomon and Baruch Nevo (Mahwah, NJ: Lawrence Erlbaum Associates, Publishers, 2002), 89–107.

28. Ramzi Suleiman, "Planned Encounters Between Jewish and Palestinian Israelis: A Social-Psychological Perspective," *Journal of Social Issues* 60, no. 2 (2004): 323–37.

29. R. Ben-Ari and Y. Amir , "Imutim ben kvutsot byisrael—Haarachat matsav venitive shenuy" [Intergroup Confrontations in Israel: Assessment and Paths of Change], *Psychologia* 1 (1988) 49–57, as reported by Suleiman.

30. Ifat Maoz, "Dialogue and Social Justice in Workshops of Jews and Arabs in Israel," in *The Psychology of Resolving Global Conflicts: From War to Peace,* Vol. 2, ed. Mari Fitzduff and Chris Stout (Westport, CT: Praeger Security International, 2006), xl, 133–46, 250.

31. Ifat Maoz and others, "Learning About 'Good Enough' Through 'Bad Enough': A Story of a Planned Dialogue Between Israeli Jews and Palestinians," *Human Relations* 57, no. 9 (2004): 1075–101.

32. Ifat Maoz, "Coexistence is in the Eye of the Beholder: Evaluating Intergroup Encounter Interventions Between Jews and Arabs in Israel," *Journal of Social Issues* 60, no. 2 (2004): 437–52.

33. Ifat Maoz, "Power Relations in Intergroup Encounters: A Case Study of Jewish-Arab Encounters in Israel," *International Journal of Intercultural Relations* 24, no. 2 (2000): 259–77.

34. Ifat Maoz, "Peace-Building With the Hawks: Attitude Change of Jewish-Israeli Hawks and Doves Following Dialogue Encounters With Palestinians," *International Journal of Intercultural Relations* 27, no. 6 (2003): 701–14.

35. David Bargal, "Structure and Process in Reconciliation-Transformation Workshops: Encounters Between Israeli and Palestinian Youth," *Small Group Research* 35, no. 5 (2004): 596–616.

36. Shifra Sagy, Shoshana Steinberg, and Mouin Faheraladin, "The Personal Self and the Collective Self in Group Encounters Between Jews and Arabs in Israel: Two Intervention Strategies," *Megamot* 41, no. 4 (2002): 534–56.

37. Ben Mollov and Chaim Lavie, "Culture, Dialogue, and Perception Change in the Israeli-Palestinian Conflict," *International Journal of Conflict Management* 12, no. 1 (2001): 69–87.

38. Zvi Bekerman, "Can Education Contribute to Coexistence and Reconciliation? Religious and National Ceremonies in Bilingual Palestinian-Jewish Schools in Israel," *Peace & Conflict: Journal of Peace Psychology* 8, no. 3 (2002): 259–76.

39. Charlotte F. Cole, Cairo Arafat, and Chava Tidhar, "The Educational Impact of *Rechov Sumsum/Shara'a Simsim:* A Sesame Street Television Series to Promote Respect and Understanding Among Children Living in Israel, the West Bank and Gaza," *International Journal of Behavioral Development* 27, no. 5 (2003): 409–22.

40. Abraham Fund, "Survey on Coexistence Organizations and Activities in Israel" (paper presented at the first meeting of the Civic Rights Forum, Tel Aviv, Israel, March 2002).

41. Grace Feuerverger, "Oasis of Peace: A Community of Moral Education in Israel," *Journal of Moral Education* 24, no. 2 (1995): 113–41; Grace Feuerverger, "An Educational Program for Peace: Jewish-Arab Conflict Resolution in Israel," *Theory into Practice* 36, no. 1 (1997): 17–25; Grace Feuerverger, "Neve Shalom/Wahat Al-Salam: A Jewish-Arab School for Peace," *Teachers College Record* 99, no. 4 (1998): 692–730.

42. Jocelyn Anne Glazier, "Developing Cultural Fluency: Arab and Jewish Students Engaging in One Another's Company," *Harvard Educational Review* 73, no. 2 (2003): 141–63.

43. http://www.handinhand12.org/.

44. Marwan Dwairy, "Culturally Sensitive Education: Adapting Self-Oriented Assertiveness Training to Collective Minorities," *Journal of Social Issues* 60, no. 2 (2004): 423–36.

45. Michelle Slone, Ricardo Tarrasch, and Dana Hallis, "Ethnic Stereotypic Attitudes Among Israeli Children: Two Intervention Programs," *Merrill-Palmer Quarterly* 46, no. 2 (2000): 370–89.

46. Rachel Hertz-Lazarowitz, "Existence and Coexistence in Acre: The Power of Educational Activism," *Journal of Social Issues* 60, no. 2 (2004): 357–71.

47. Isabel Kershner, "Walking the Line," *Jerusalem Report,* September 18, 2006, 22.

48. Gavriel Salomon, "Does Peace Education Make a Difference in the Context of an Intractable Conflict?" *Peace & Conflict: Journal of Peace Psychology* 10, no. 3 (2004): 257–74.

49. Paulo Freire, *Pedagogy of the Oppressed* (New York: Continuum, 1999).

50. B. McCombs and J. Whisler, *The Learner-Centered Classroom and School: Strategies for Increasing Student Motivation and Achievement* (San Francisco, CA: The Jossey-Bass Education Series, 1997).

51. Svi Shapiro, "Toward a Critical Pedagogy of Peace Education," in *Peace Education: The Concept, Principles, and Practices Around the World*, ed. Gavriel Salomon and Baruch Nevo (Mahwah, NJ: Lawrence Erlbaum Associates, Publishers, 2002), 63–71.

52. E. Aronson and S. Patnoe, *The Jigsaw Classroom: Building Cooperation in the Classroom*, 2nd ed. (New York: Addison Wesley Longman, 1997); E. Aronson and A. Gonzalez, "Desegregation, Jigsaw, and the Mexican-American Experience," in *Eliminating Racism: Profiles in Controversy*, ed. P.A. Katz and D.A. Taylor (New York, NY: Plenum Press, 1988), 301–14; I. Walker and M. Crogan, "Academic Performance, Prejudice, and the Jigsaw Classroom: New Pieces to the Puzzle," *Journal of Community and Applied Social Psychology* 8 (1998): 381–93; E. Aronson, "Building Empathy, Compassion and Achievement in the Jigsaw Classroom," in *Improving Academic Achievement: Impact of Psychological Factors on Education*, ed. J. Aronson (Boston, MA: Academic Press, 2002), 213–24.

53. S. Kenan, "Reconsidering Peace and Multicultural Education After 9/11: The Case of Educational Outreach for Muslim Sensitivity Curriculum in New York City," *Educational Sciences: Theory & Practice* 5, no. 1 (2005): 172–80.

54. M.F. Salinas and J. Garr, "Effect of Learner-Centered Classrooms and Schools on Literacy Rate and Academic Performance of Minority and Non-Minority Groups," submitted for publication.

INTERVIEWS

An Interview with Abu Muhammad, Who Lives in Gaza. Interviewer:
Shanni Masad

Abu Muhammad is in his mid-fifties and has been a blue-collar worker all his life. He is married with a large family, and for many years, he worked in Israel in close contact with Israeli managers and coworkers. Currently, his son is undergoing cancer treatment in a major hospital near Tel Aviv.

Interviewer: Tell me a little bit about yourself.

Abu Muhammad: My name is Abu Muhammad. I live in Gaza next to the sea. I have a wife and six children, three boys and three girls. For many years I worked in Israel in the nickel plating industry and in a number of other metal-orientated factories. For the past five years since the start of Intifada I no longer work in Israel. Instead I have all sorts of business in Gaza.

Interviewer: Please tell me how did you end up, you and your son, in this hospital.

Abu Muhammad: Mohammad is my eldest son. He is 14 years old. About two years ago he started to talk about acute back pain and also to complain about his vision. I did take him to a local doctor from the Palestine Authority, and he told me that he suffers bone marrow cancer. Because I wanted him to get a better treatment, I took him to Egypt in order for him to undergo a surgery. They removed the tumor, and after that we returned home. He was fine for a while but after eight months he started to complain again about headaches and nausea. I took him once more to the doctor and he said that the cancer had returned this time to his brain. This time I decided to take him to the hospital in Israel because I have some connections and they gave me permission to arrange for an entry permit. I brought him here to Ichilov Hospital where he received ten treatments of radiation. Now I am waiting so he can receive another ten treatments. Meanwhile I sit here and worry about him so much. I just pray that he will be healthy.

Interviewer: How long have you been at the hospital already?

Abu Muhammad: For two months. Since we got here we have not returned home. I cannot leave the hospital because I don't have papers to move around outside but also because I really can't get far away from the oncology department because of my son.

Interviewer: Did you have previous relationships, before you came to the hospital, with Israelis?

Abu Muhammad: Yeah, I worked for almost thirty years in Israel, in the nickel industry and also in a glass factory with Israelis.

Interviewer: What was your relationship with those Israelis you worked with?

Abu Muhammad: Well they were my friends...work friends. I had an Israeli boss and also there were Israelis who worked with me. We would chat at work, we would laugh, but afterward I would go back home to Gaza to my family. That was during the period in which it was rather easy to enter and exit Israel...some of them I knew real well and some of them less, but they never were friends like the good friends from home.

Interviewer: So what are your feelings toward them?

Abu Muhammad: They were OK. I thought they were nice people.

Interviewer: Did you keep in touch with them after you stopped working in Israel?

Abu Muhammad: No, I never had a chance to visit Israel anymore until I came here with Mohammad. Only from my boss I would hear every few months. He would call and ask me, "how are you doing?" and "how is the family doing?"

Interviewer: How did they treat you here at the hospital?

Abu Muhammad: When I first got here, Mohammad was already very ill, and here everybody tried to help him. They gave him a wonderful service. Also, before my friends from work would help me if I ever needed something, but they knew me for many many years. Here, even though they really did not know me or Mohammad, they helped and not only the doctors also Eti, the woman in charge of the children's area of the oncology department, and all the volunteers who always come and ask me how am I doing and how is Mohammad doing. They worry about him.

Interviewer: Did you develop any personal relationships with Israelis at the time you have been at the hospital?

Abu Muhammad: Look there was here another family that also had a child who was really ill. I would sit mainly with his father and talk to him you know, about the worries and the hopes. He was really nice and also his wife. I also know you, you come and talk to me every time you visit. There are other volunteers, and all of them come, they say "hello," they sit with me and talk, and we chat about stuff.

Interviewer: From your personal conversation with Israelis that you have met, are there any new things that you learned about them?

Abu Muhammad: Look, with everybody I talked about different stuff. But I did meet here other people whose children who are sick, and I saw that they want for their children that I want for my children. They want them to get a good education, a good job, to marry. It is not that different than us. . . all the time it looks like we are so far away from each other but I did see that when your son is sick, for everybody it is the same priorities, just to be in good health. Me too I just want that my children will be healthy.

Interviewer: Did your opinion about Israelis differ from the ones that you had before Mohammad was admitted to the hospital?

Abu Muhammad: I don't know. When I took Mohammad from Gaza to Israel, everybody told me, "What are you doing? Why are you taking him there? They are just going to make you trouble." Everybody said that the best thing would be to take him back to Egypt. But I knew that the doctors here are much better, so insisted. Really they didn't make any trouble for me here. I saw that they really want to help. They behave toward Mohammad just like everybody else, and they are worried about him all the time. And they worry about me too. People come to play with Mohammad to do activities with him, they come and ask how am I doing and how am I feeling. Even my friends who worked with me once, the Israelis, came to visit Mohammad, I was really moved. I did not think that something like this could happen.

Interviewer: So what do you think today about the Israel–Palestine conflict? Have your opinions changed since you came to the hospital?

Abu Muhammad: Look I've always thought that we need to make peace. Enough is enough; both you and us are suffering from this, the way the situation is today. We must fix this situation together. We have a number of problems, and the only way we can solve them is through peace. After

I have been here for a long time, I believe that, if other people, friends of mine, would see how they are behaving toward my son and me, they would not have told me not to bring him here. Maybe I will then even send you and other people like you to us, so they could see that we also behave nicely with honor and respect. You think about us that we are a certain way and a lot of people among us say: the Jews they only make trouble. People must stop thinking that way.

Interviewer: So do you have a different way of solving the conflict?

Abu Muhammad: I do hope so. Both sides often do things that are not nice one to the other. You do not allow us to go to work and make a living. Our side also does not always do good things. I believe that our leaders have to sit down and solve the conflict. I think that everybody wants peace, both peoples. And it is the leadership job to help. Maybe if they will see that everyone can help the other, the way they are helping my son, and we can get along together it will be a lot easier to do it. They will begin to think positive things and be scared less from each other.

An Interview with Yoav, Who Lives in Haifa. Interviewers: Adi Bar-Oz
and Moran Ben Sara

Yoav is 36 years old, married with a young daughter. He is a software engineer and also an activist in the Peace Now movement. The interview was completed two days after two Israeli soldiers were kidnapped by Hezbollah in Lebanon and when the Israeli air offensive was just beginning.

Interviewer: Why don't you start about telling me about yourself?

Yoav: My name is Yoav, I am 36 years old, married for eight years to Haddas and father to Noam, she is 4 years old. I live in the northern Israeli city of Haifa and work for a high-tech company.

Interviewer: I understand that you support the "Peace Now" movement. Can you tell me a little bit about it?

Yoav: The Peace Now movement is a nonpartisan movement that belongs to the Zionist left in Israel. The movements' aspiration is to achieve peace, compromise, reconciliation with the Palestine people. The movement was founded in the year 1978 and the principal goal is to gather public support for the peace process even if the price is concessions of territories from the State of Israel. Because I belong to this group I support the establishment of the Palestinian state next to the State of Israel. We have a number of basic principles, for example, the right of Israel to secure borders and the right of our neighbors, the Palestine's, for self-determination. The Oslo Agreement, which was signed in 1993, it's in my view a breakthrough in the peace process and my support and that of all others who support the agreement is complete. We will support every step that will be made to advance the end of this terrible conflict. For years we always pressured and will continue to pressure the parties in power to take the initiative and take steps to end the occupation and to enter negotiations for peace. From the beginning of a road we claimed that the continuation of the occupation of the Gaza Strip goes against peace. We are active all around the country, and we use advertising and public campaigns. We distribute the explanatory declarations and flyers to the citizens. I aspire to continue calling for the government to reach a compromise agreement with the Palestinians because I don't want to sacrifice my life and the life of my children. Our life is a lot more important than war or a fight over territories, which do not contribute anything to the country. In my view the settlers (in the occupied Palestine territories) can stay living in the territories but that should not come at the expense of the rest of the people who are interested in a quiet and peaceful life and not more war. We must trust the Palestine people, they are not all the same, most of them believe in peace and want it.

Interviewer: Why did you join this group, why do you support this position?

Yoav: I joined the movement after my military service. In the army I was a combat solider in the Egoz unit (an elite commando unit) and I participated in not a few very hard operations that brought to a great number of deaths for both sides. After my service and after I lost many good friends I reach the conclusion that only through compromise with the Palestine people we can accomplish a better future and security. The State of Israel should not think about who is right, it has to reach a compromise and end the conflict. I must emphasize that in order for us to be able to live here with peace and quiet, we must reach recognition of and understanding with the Palestine people, that they also deserve a sovereign country. They are a nation just like we are and we all deserve a state and the land where we can live in safety. We must trust them. There are certain people in this country who have a certain opinion about the Arabs and they are not willing to try and recognize the Arabs. They think that if an Arab carried out a terrorist action, then all of them do and that is not correct. If we trust them everything will look different. I believe that there has to be mutual recognition and that means that both peoples have to live a national life complete in their own countries and only that way the life of each one of these peoples will be better. We need to respect their desire to establish a state and a leadership.

Interviewer: Allow me to ask about the Palestine–Israel conflict. What do you think?

Yoav: The conflict began many years ago and not many governments in our country have made an effort to end it. The conflict was unnecessary and began because of extremist opinions on both sides. Extremists don't have a place in the delegations that deal with the conflict. We are a country and we need to think with logic and not fanatism. We need to remember that the Arabs are people too just like us full of beliefs and like us there are extremists amongst them. We must remember that not all of them are the same. If you ask me, I believe that the majority of the Arabs are good people that are interested in a quiet life and are not in favor of death and violence. I think that we are obligated to end the conflict that exists between us for many years already. The departing point for a permanent agreement in the Israel–Palestine conflict is mutual recognition and the right of both peoples to a full national life, each one in its own sovereign land. In order to advance peace and reconciliation between both nations, Israel must adopt some principles, that will be difficult to accept for most people and I will explain some of them right now. One of the principles is that the Palestine people have the right for self-determination including the right to establish their own country next to the State of Israel. Israel settlers whose settlements will be located, after we determine the permanent borders, in the territories in the Palestine state, will have to evacuate the houses, because we will not be able to reach a permanent agreement if we do not evacuate the settlements. Of course Jerusalem will remain a united city and will not be divided. These are the main principles, there are some other principles that I will not explain here. The conflict in my view is a conflict that is accompanied with blood, death, and so on. In summary what I would like to emphasize that in order for us to live our lives in peace and quiet and that less soldiers will have to sacrifice their life, a Palestine state must be established and that will bring quiet to the region.

Interviewer: What do you think will be the ultimate solution?

Yoav: I will return to the things that I said in the previous questions. In order to end this difficult and long conflict, Israel must exit the occupied territories and a Palestine state has to be established. There has to be mutual recognition of both peoples: the people of Israel and the people of Palestine. Only that way we could live in peace. Over the years Israel has taken some important steps in order to minimize the conflict, the first one of them was the withdrawal from Lebanon (in 2000) that happened about six years ago. We withdrew from Lebanon and the policy of restraint that we had for six years brought international support for Israel. A support that probably we would not have received before that. Today we earned support from one side to the other from the countries who have influence in the world, that is because of the knowledge that we were attacked from inside a sovereign country without any provocation. Another important step that the country did was the engagement (from the Gaza Strip). The completion of the engagement program, the evacuation of the settlements, and the withdrawal of the Israel Defense Forces from Gaza and the northern Samaria opened an opportunity window to renew the peace process and created a new reality for the people of Israel and the people of Palestine. This engagement program proved once and for all that the Israel society is ready and capable of undertaking a process of evacuating settlements. The completion of the disengagement program for Israel and the Palestine is a new political horizon and an opportunity window to restart the diplomatic negotiation and renew the peace process. In order to continue with these positive dynamists in the region, both sides must undertake a number of political and security steps, in addition to the renewal of the dialogued channels and the attempts to reach a peace agreement that can be and happen only after a compromise. I think that the State of Israel must continue additional steps until we reach a solution to the conflict. In my opinion, and the opinion of the movement I am a member of, the most important of these steps is a sovereign state for the Palestine people. We must recognize them and they will recognize us and then everything will be a lot simpler.

Interviewer: Is there anything else you would like to add?

Yoav: Yes, I would like to say to all who are reading this and think that I am naïve to liberal or any other thoughts; that in all the years that we have had the current policy, we have lost a great number of people (soldiers, innocent civilians); in order for these terrible losses to end, we must reach a compromise and peace with our neighbors. Human life is the most important thing for all of us, we have to take care of ourselves and we can do that a lot better and a lot safer if we separate from our neighbors, and to every nation there will be a sovereign state. I know and understand that the people who will read these things will oppose them, but I do believe that every one of us has to take a few minutes, look inside ourselves, and think if it is not worth it to end this difficult conflict, so the lives of the people and the citizens of this country will be safer and better.

EPILOGUE

I was trying to think of an appropriate metaphor for the Israeli–Palestinian conflict, and I had this idea. A brave group of soldiers is entrusted with the protection of a very precious jewel. At first, they just warded the jewel with their weapons and bodies, but as it became clear that the threat could be greater, they started to build a fortification around it. As the years passed, they recruited more and more soldiers, built state-of-the-art defenses, and strengthened their increasing layers of fortification around it. This dynamic continued for generations, until one day a more powerful army was able to defeat them and break through the fortifications. When they reached the inner sanctum, the resting place of the precious jewel, they found it empty. "How can this be?" they asked. It was simple, at one point in time, the only way the guarding soldiers could keep affording to recruit more conscripts and build more defenses was to sell the jewel. The jewel lost its importance because its protection became a way of life that needed to be preserved, even at the price of its *raison d'etre*.

The Israeli–Palestinian conflict has a very similar dynamic. Both Palestinians and Israelis fight to preserve their ancient cultures, their way of life, and the inalienable national right to pursue peace and prosperity. However, the battle has become more important than its goals. Defeating the hated enemy becomes a goal in and of itself, and both peoples are willing to sacrifice their values and their lives in order to just "win" the struggle, losing sight of what the purpose of fighting originally was. This is a conflict that has lasted already, one way or another, over one century. And some people believe and are prepared for it to last for ever. Some, like columnist Bradley Burston, of the *Haaretz* daily, even talk about a "Peace Never" movement that plagues both Palestinians and Israelis because it serves those who thrive in the status quo and because it is easier and more comfortable to live in the known reality than to leap into new attempts at peace that might end, once more, only in bigger disappointment and bigger bloodshed.

What people who believe in the status quo and a passive approach to the conflict don't realize is that time is running out, for both Palestinians and Israelis, to achieve a just, negotiated solution to the conflict that will bring lasting peace, and eventually, good relationships between the neighboring countries. Time is running out not only because the killing of every Palestinian or Israeli child in this senseless conflict is a crime, nor because so many people have to live day to day with fear and anxiety. For the Palestinians, time is running out because the older generation, the one who actually worked in Israel and speaks Hebrew and can become the bridge between the two cultures, is getting older, losing its cultural and moral dominance and its influence among young Palestinians. The Palestinians are known in the Arab world for their intellectual development and were considered educated, tolerant, and refined. However, life under occupation has bred a new generation of young people who care more about war and martyrdom, and slowly, the old values of education and tolerance are being replaced as the core of the Palestinian ethos. If the war is not stopped soon, the Palestinians will metamorphose from a people of the book to a people of the rifle, who will keep fighting just because it is the only thing they know.

For the Israelis, time is running out not only because the occupation is similarly eroding its core values but also because the current situation has been sustainable only because the world powers are willing to allow it to continue. In the United States there are slightly over five million Jews today. The number was six million thirty years ago. It is estimated that there are over six million Muslims in the United States, already more than the Jews. However, if demographic trends continue, in twenty years there would be four million Jews and ten million Muslims. Politicians have no friends, they only have interests, and time for Israel to reach a negotiated solution is running out because, I have no doubt, support from the world superpower will diminish too when politicians have to face ten million Muslim voters against four million Jewish ones.

Throughout this book, we have discussed how the obstacles to achieving peace are more psychological than political, how perception is more important than reality, and how stereotypes and misconceptions can lead to a lot of pain and suffering. Because of this pain, of this hatred, a lot of people have developed a sense of helplessness, and they look at any excuse they have to insist on "not recognizing" each other, not having "dialogue" with each other, and not being "a partner for peace." Many well-intentioned people on both sides and in the international community think that boycotts, blockades, embargoes, and so forth can help, but they don't. They just make each side raise its defenses, and psychologically, give them one more reason to confirm their self-serving bias that "the world is against us." All of these have made it harder, not easier, to achieve peace.

Furthermore, psychological and social research has clearly shown that, even if a solution is hard to reach, there are many avenues that we could use to inch closer to reconciliation. We can reduce stereotypes through education, through constructive uses of the media, and through the building of common projects. We can reduce extremism by removing its social support, by delegitimizing violence, and by looking at military options as a sad choice made out of "lack of options" instead of something we should glorify and be proud of. We can increase dialogue by shedding zero-sum negotiating tactics in favor of cooperative problem-solving task forces. And we can concentrate our efforts to achieve peace at building bridges instead of bombing them. None of these things will give us the certainty of peace, but they will definitely bring us closer. And even if reconciliation is far away and the road is long and treacherous, we certainly will never make it there as long as we advocate just staying put, doing nothing, and waiting for a miracle to occur.

The irony is, then, that even if a solution is not at hand, there is a lot more that can be done to reduce stereotypes, to stifle extremism, and to minimize pain. There is a lot more that can be done to promote peace and foster reconciliation. There is a lot more that can be done, and if there is, it is our moral responsibility to stand up and do it.

APPENDIX:
THE GENEVA ACCORD
A MODEL ISRAELI–PALESTINIAN
PEACE AGREEMENT*

The State of Israel (hereinafter "Israel") and the Palestine Liberation Organization (hereinafter "PLO"), the representative of the Palestinian people (hereinafter the "Parties"):

Reaffirming their determination to put an end to decades of confrontation and conflict and to live in peaceful coexistence, mutual dignity, and security based on a just, lasting, and comprehensive peace and achieving historic reconciliation;

Recognizing that peace requires the transition from the logic of war and confrontation to the logic of peace and cooperation and that acts and words characteristic of the state of war are neither appropriate nor acceptable in the era of peace;

Affirming their deep belief that the logic of peace requires compromise and that the only viable solution is a two-state solution based on UNSC Resolution 242 and 338;

Affirming that this agreement marks the recognition of the right of the Jewish people to statehood and the recognition of the right of the Palestinian people to statehood, without prejudice to the equal rights of the Parties' respective citizens;

Recognizing that after years of living in mutual fear and insecurity, both peoples need to enter an era of peace, security, and stability, entailing all necessary actions by the Parties to guarantee the realization of this era;

*From http://www.geneva-accord.org.

Recognizing each other's right to peaceful and secure existence within secure and recognized boundaries free from threats or acts of force;

Determined to establish relations based on cooperation and the commitment to live side by side as good neighbors aiming both separately and jointly to contribute to the well-being of their peoples;

Reaffirming their obligation to conduct themselves in conformity with the norms of international law and the Charter of the United Nations;

Confirming that this Agreement is concluded within the framework of the Middle East peace process initiated in Madrid in October 1991, the Declaration of Principles of September 13, 1993, the subsequent agreements including the Interim Agreement of September 1995, the Wye River Memorandum of October 1998, and the Sharm El-Sheikh Memorandum of September 4, 1999, and the permanent status negotiations including the Camp David Summit of July 2000, the Clinton Ideas of December 2000, and the Taba Negotiations of January 2001;

Reiterating their commitment to United Nations Security Council Resolutions 242, 338, and 1397 and confirming their understanding that this Agreement is based on, will lead to, and—by its fulfillment—will constitute the full implementation of these resolutions and to the settlement of the Israeli–Palestinian conflict in all its aspects;

Declaring that this Agreement constitutes the realization of the permanent status peace component envisaged in President Bush's speech of June 24, 2002, and in the Quartet Roadmap process.

Declaring that this Agreement marks the historic reconciliation between the Palestinians and the Israelis and paves the way to reconciliation between the Arab world and Israel and the establishment of normal, peaceful relations between the Arab states and Israel in accordance with the relevant clauses of the Beirut Arab League Resolution of March 28, 2002; and

Resolved to pursue the goal of attaining a comprehensive regional peace, thus contributing to stability, security, development, and prosperity throughout the region;

Have agreed on the following:

Article 1—Purpose of the Permanent Status Agreement

1. The Permanent Status Agreement (hereinafter "this Agreement") ends the era of conflict and ushers in a new era based on peace, cooperation, and good neighborly relations between the Parties.

2. The implementation of this Agreement will settle all the claims of the Parties arising from events occurring prior to its signature. No further claims related to events prior to this Agreement may be raised by either Party.

Article 2—Relations between the Parties

1. The state of Israel shall recognize the state of Palestine (hereinafter "Palestine") upon its establishment. The state of Palestine shall immediately recognize the state of Israel.
2. The state of Palestine shall be the successor to the PLO with all its rights and obligations.
3. Israel and Palestine shall immediately establish full diplomatic and consular relations with each other and will exchange resident Ambassadors, within one month of their mutual recognition.
4. The Parties recognize Palestine and Israel as the homelands of their respective peoples. The Parties are committed not to interfere in each other's internal affairs.
5. This Agreement supercedes all prior agreements between the Parties.
6. Without prejudice to the commitments undertaken by them in this Agreement, relations between Israel and Palestine shall be based upon the provisions of the Charter of the United Nations.
7. With a view to the advancement of the relations between the two states and peoples, Palestine and Israel shall cooperate in areas of common interest. These shall include, but are not limited to, dialogue between their legislatures and state institutions, cooperation between their appropriate local authorities, promotion of nongovernmental civil society cooperation, and joint programs and exchange in the areas of culture, media, youth, science, education, environment, health, agriculture, tourism, and crime prevention. The Israeli-Palestinian Cooperation Committee will oversee this cooperation in accordance with Article 8.
8. The Parties shall cooperate in areas of joint economic interest, to best realize the human potential of their respective peoples. In this regard, they will work bilaterally, regionally, and with the international community to maximize the benefit of peace to the broadest cross-section of their respective populations. Relevant standing bodies shall be established by the Parties to this effect.
9. The Parties shall establish robust modalities for security cooperation and engage in a comprehensive and uninterrupted effort to end terrorism and violence directed against each other's persons, property, institutions,

or territory. This effort shall continue at all times and shall be insulated from any possible crises and other aspects of the Parties' relations.

10. Israel and Palestine shall work together and separately with other parties in the region to enhance and promote regional cooperation and coordination in spheres of common interest.

11. The Parties shall establish a ministerial-level Palestinian-Israeli High Steering Committee to guide, monitor, and facilitate the process of implementation of this Agreement, both bilaterally and in accordance with the mechanisms in Article 3 hereunder.

Article 3—Implementation and Verification Group

1. Establishment and Composition

i. An Implementation and Verification Group (IVG) shall hereby be established to facilitate, assist in, guarantee, monitor, and resolve disputes relating to the implementation of this Agreement.

ii. The IVG shall include the United States, the Russian Federation, the European Union, the United Nations, and other parties, both regional and international, to be agreed on by the Parties.

iii. The IVG shall work in coordination with the Palestinian-Israeli High Steering Committee established in Article 2/11 above and subsequent to that with the Israeli-Palestinian Cooperation Committee (IPCC) established in Article 8 hereunder.

iv. The structure, procedures, and modalities of the IVG are set forth below and detailed in Annex X.

2. Structure

i. A senior political-level contact group (Contact Group), composed of all the IVG members, shall be the highest authority in the IVG.

ii. The Contact Group shall appoint, in consultation with the Parties, a Special Representative who will be the principal executive of the IVG on the ground. The Special Representative shall manage the work of the IVG and maintain constant contact with the Parties, the Palestinian-Israeli High Steering Committee, and the Contact Group.

iii. The IVG permanent headquarters and secretariat shall be based in an agreed upon location in Jerusalem.

iv. The IVG shall establish its bodies referred to in this Agreement and additional bodies as it deems necessary. These bodies shall be an integral part of and under the authority of the IVG.

v. The Multinational Force (MF) established under Article 5 shall be an integral part of the IVG. The Special Representative shall, subject to the approval of the Parties, appoint the Commander of the MF who shall be responsible for the daily command of the MF. Details relating to the Special Representative and MF Force Commander are set forth in Annex X.

vi. The IVG shall establish a dispute settlement mechanism, in accordance with Article 16.

3. Coordination with the Parties

A Trilateral Committee composed of the Special Representative and the Palestinian-Israeli High Steering Committee shall be established and shall meet on at least a monthly basis to review the implementation of this Agreement. The Trilateral Committee will convene within 48 hours upon the request of any of the three parties represented.

4. Functions

In addition to the functions specified elsewhere in this Agreement, the IVG shall:

i. Take appropriate measures based on the reports it receives from the MF,

ii. Assist the Parties in implementing the Agreement and preempt and promptly mediate disputes on the ground.

5. Termination

In accordance with the progress in the implementation of this Agreement, and with the fulfillment of the specific mandated functions, the IVG shall terminate its activities in the said spheres. The IVG shall continue to exist unless otherwise agreed by the Parties.

Article 4—Territory

1. The International Borders between the States of Palestine and Israel

i. In accordance with UNSC Resolutions 242 and 338, the border between the states of Palestine and Israel shall be based on the June 4th 1967 lines with reciprocal modifications on a 1:1 basis as set forth in attached Map 1.

ii. The Parties recognize the border, as set out in attached Map 1, as the permanent, secure, and recognized international boundary between them.

2. Sovereignty and Inviolability

i. The Parties recognize and respect each other's sovereignty, territorial integrity, and political independence, as well as the inviolability of each other's territory, including territorial waters and airspace. They shall respect this inviolability in accordance with this Agreement, the UN Charter, and other rules of international law.

ii. The Parties recognize each other's rights in their exclusive economic zones in accordance with international law.

3. Israeli Withdrawal

i. Israel shall withdraw in accordance with Article 5.

ii. Palestine shall assume responsibility for the areas from which Israel withdraws.

iii. The transfer of authority from Israel to Palestine shall be in accordance with Annex X.

iv. The IVG shall monitor, verify, and facilitate the implementation of this Article.

4. Demarcation

i. A Joint Technical Border Commission (Commission) composed of the two Parties shall be established to conduct the technical demarcation of the border in accordance with this Article. The procedures governing the work of this Commission are set forth in Annex X.

ii. Any disagreement in the Commission shall be referred to the IVG in accordance with Annex X.

iii. The physical demarcation of the international borders shall be completed by the Commission not later than nine months from the date of the entry into force of this Agreement.

5. Settlements

i. The state of Israel shall be responsible for resettling the Israelis residing in Palestinian sovereign territory outside this territory.

ii. The resettlement shall be completed according to the schedule stipulated in Article 5.

iii. Existing arrangements in the West Bank and Gaza Strip regarding Israeli settlers and settlements, including security, shall remain in force in each of the settlements until the date prescribed in the timetable for the completion of the evacuation of the relevant settlement.

iv. Modalities for the assumption of authority over settlements by Palestine are set forth in Annex X. The IVG shall resolve any disputes that may arise during its implementation.

v. Israel shall keep intact the immovable property, infrastructure, and facilities in Israeli settlements to be transferred to Palestinian sovereignty. An agreed inventory shall be drawn up by the Parties with the IVG in advance of the completion of the evacuation and in accordance with Annex X.

vi. The state of Palestine shall have exclusive title to all land and any buildings, facilities, infrastructure, or other property remaining in any of the settlements on the date prescribed in the timetable for the completion of the evacuation of this settlement.

6. Corridor

i. The states of Palestine and Israel shall establish a corridor linking the West Bank and Gaza Strip. This corridor shall:

   a. Be under Israeli sovereignty.

   b. Be permanently open.

   c. Be under Palestinian administration in accordance with Annex X of this Agreement. Palestinian law shall apply to persons using and procedures appertaining to the corridor.

   d. Not disrupt Israeli transportation and other infrastructural networks, or endanger the environment, public safety, or public health. Where necessary, engineering solutions will be sought to avoid such disruptions.

   e. Allow for the establishment of the necessary infrastructural facilities linking the West Bank and the Gaza Strip. Infrastructural facilities shall be understood to include, inter alia, pipelines, electrical and communications cables, and associated equipment as detailed in Annex X.

   f. Not be used in contravention of this Agreement.

ii. Defensive barriers shall be established along the corridor and Palestinians shall not enter Israel from this corridor, nor shall Israelis enter Palestine from the corridor.

iii. The Parties shall seek the assistance of the international community in securing the financing for the corridor.

iv. The IVG shall guarantee the implementation of this Article in accordance with Annex X.

v. Any disputes arising between the Parties from the operation of the corridor shall be resolved in accordance with Article 16.

vi. The arrangements set forth in this clause may only be terminated or revised by agreement of both Parties.

Article 5—Security

1. General Security Provisions

The Parties acknowledge that mutual understanding and cooperation in security-related matters will form a significant part of their bilateral relations and will further enhance regional security. Palestine and Israel shall base their security relations on cooperation, mutual trust, good neighborly relations, and the protection of their joint interests.
Palestine and Israel each shall

a. recognize and respect the other's right to live in peace within secured and recognized boundaries free from the threat or acts of war, terrorism, and violence;

b. refrain from the threat or use of force against the territorial integrity or political independence of the other and shall settle all disputes between them by peaceful means;

c. refrain from joining, assisting, promoting, or cooperating with any coalition, organization, or alliance of a military or security character, the objectives or activities of which include launching aggression or other acts of hostility against the other;

d. refrain from organizing, encouraging, or allowing the formation of irregular forces or armed bands, including mercenaries and militias, within their respective territory and prevent their establishment. In this respect, any existing irregular forces or armed bands shall be disbanded and prevented from reforming at any future date;

e. refrain from organizing, assisting, allowing, or participating in acts of violence in or against the other or acquiescing in activities directed toward the commission of such acts.

To further security cooperation, the Parties shall establish a high-level Joint Security Committee that shall meet on at least a monthly basis.

The Joint Security Committee shall have a permanent joint office and may establish such subcommittees as it deems necessary, including sub-committees to immediately resolve localized tensions.

2. Regional Security

Israel and Palestine shall work together with their neighbors and the international community to build a secure and stable Middle East, free from weapons of mass destruction, both conventional and nonconventional, in the context of a comprehensive, lasting, and stable peace, characterized by reconciliation, goodwill, and the renunciation of the use of force.

To this end, the Parties shall work together to establish a regional security regime.

3. Defense Characteristics of the Palestinian State

No armed forces, other than as specified in this Agreement, will be deployed or stationed in Palestine.

Palestine shall be a nonmilitarized state, with a strong security force. Accordingly, the limitations on the weapons that may be purchased, owned, or used by the Palestinian Security Force (PSF) or manufactured in Palestine shall be specified in Annex X. Any proposed changes to Annex X shall be considered by a trilateral committee composed of the two Parties and the MF. If no agreement is reached in the trilateral committee, the IVG may make its own recommendations.

a. No individuals or organizations in Palestine other than the PSF and the organs of the IVG, including the MF, may purchase, possess, carry, or use weapons except as provided by law.

The PSF shall

a. maintain border control;

b. maintain law-and-order and perform police functions;

c. perform intelligence and security functions;

d. prevent terrorism;

e. conduct rescue and emergency missions; and

f. supplement essential community services when necessary.

The MF shall monitor and verify compliance with this clause.

4. Terrorism

The Parties reject and condemn terrorism and violence in all its forms and shall pursue public policies accordingly. In addition, the parties shall refrain from actions and policies that are liable to nurture extremism and create conditions conducive to terrorism on either side.

The Parties shall take joint and, in their respective territories, unilateral comprehensive and continuous efforts against all aspects of violence and terrorism. These efforts shall include the prevention and preemption of such acts and the prosecution of their perpetrators.

To that end, the Parties shall maintain ongoing consultation, cooperation, and exchange of information between their respective security forces.

A Trilateral Security Committee composed of the two Parties and the United States shall be formed to ensure the implementation of this Article. The Trilateral Security Committee shall develop comprehensive policies and guidelines to fight terrorism and violence.

5. Incitement

Without prejudice to freedom of expression and other internationally recognized human rights, Israel and Palestine shall promulgate laws to prevent incitement to irredentism, racism, terrorism, and violence and vigorously enforce them.

The IVG shall assist the Parties in establishing guidelines for the implementation of this clause and shall monitor the Parties' adherence thereto.

6. Multinational Force

A Multinational Force (MF) shall be established to provide security guarantees to the Parties, act as a deterrent, and oversee the implementation of the relevant provisions of this Agreement.

The composition, structure, and size of the MF are set forth in Annex X.

To perform the functions specified in this Agreement, the MF shall be deployed in the state of Palestine. The MF shall enter into the appropriate Status of Forces Agreement (SOFA) with the state of Palestine.

In accordance with this Agreement, and as detailed in Annex X, the MF shall

    a. In light of the nonmilitarized nature of the Palestinian state, protect the territorial integrity of the state of Palestine.

b. Serve as a deterrent against external attacks that could threaten either of the Parties.

c. Deploy observers to areas adjacent to the lines of the Israeli withdrawal during the phases of this withdrawal, in accordance with Annex X.

d. Deploy observers to monitor the territorial and maritime borders of the state of Palestine, as specified in clause 5/13.

e. Perform the functions on the Palestinian international border crossings specified in clause 5/12.

f. Perform the functions relating to the early warning stations as specified in clause 5/8.

g. Perform the functions specified in clause 5/3.

h. Perform the functions specified in clause 5/7.

i. Perform the functions specified in Article 10.

j. Help in the enforcement of antiterrorism measures.

k. Help in the training of the PSF.

In relation to the above, the MF shall report to and update the IVG in accordance with Annex X.

The MF shall only be withdrawn or have its mandate changed by agreement of the Parties.

7. Evacuation

i. Israel shall withdraw all its military and security personnel and equipment, including landmines, and all persons employed to support them, and all military installations from the territory of the state of Palestine, except as otherwise agreed in Annex X, in stages.

ii. The staged withdrawals shall commence immediately upon entry into force of this Agreement and shall be made in accordance with the timetable and modalities set forth in Annex X.

iii. The stages shall be designed subject to the following principles:

a. The need to create immediate clear contiguity and facilitate the early implementation of Palestinian development plans.

b. Israel's capacity to relocate, house, and absorb settlers. While costs and inconveniences are inherent in such a process, these shall not be unduly disruptive.

c. The need to construct and operationalize the border between the two states.

d. The introduction and effective functioning of the MF, in particular on the eastern border of the state of Palestine.

iv. Accordingly, the withdrawal shall be implemented in the following stages:

a. The first stage shall include the areas of the state of Palestine, as defined in Map X, and shall be completed within 9 months.

b. The second and third stages shall include the remainder of the territory of the state of Palestine and shall be completed within 21 months of the end of the first stage.

Israel shall complete its withdrawal from the territory of the state of Palestine within 30 months of the entry into force of this Agreement and in accordance with this Agreement.

Israel will maintain a small military presence in the Jordan Valley under the authority of the MF and be subject to the MF SOFA as detailed in Annex X for an additional 36 months. The stipulated period may be reviewed by the Parties in the event of relevant regional developments and may be altered by the Parties' consent.

In accordance with Annex X, the MF shall monitor and verify compliance with this clause.

8. Early Warning Stations

Israel may maintain two EWS in the northern and central West Bank at the locations set forth in Annex X.

The EWS shall be staffed by the minimal required number of Israeli personnel and shall occupy the minimal amount of land necessary for their operation as set forth in Annex X.

Access to the EWS will be guaranteed and escorted by the MF.

Internal security of the EWS shall be the responsibility of Israel. The perimeter security of the EWS shall be the responsibility of the MF.

The MF and the PSF shall maintain a liaison presence in the EWS.

The MF shall monitor and verify that the EWS is being used for purposes recognized by this Agreement as detailed in Annex X.

The arrangements set forth in this Article shall be subject to review in ten years, with any changes to be mutually agreed. Thereafter, there will be five-yearly reviews whereby the arrangements set forth in this Article may be extended by mutual consent.

If at any point during the period specified above a regional security regime is established, then the IVG may request that the Parties review whether to continue or revise operational uses for the EWS in light of these developments. Any such change will require the mutual consent of the Parties.

9. Airspace

Civil Aviation

a. The Parties recognize as applicable to each other the rights, privileges, and obligations provided for by the multilateral aviation agreements to which they are both party, particularly by the 1944 Convention on International Civil Aviation (The Chicago Convention) and the 1944 International Air Services Transit Agreement.

b. In addition, the Parties shall, upon entry into force of this Agreement, establish a trilateral committee composed of the two Parties and the IVG to design the most efficient management system for civil aviation, including those relevant aspects of the air traffic control system. In the absence of consensus the IVG may make its own recommendations.

Training

a. The Israeli Air Force shall be entitled to use the Palestinian sovereign airspace for training purposes in accordance with Annex X, which shall be based on rules pertaining to IAF use of Israeli airspace.

b. The IVG shall monitor and verify compliance with this clause. Either Party may submit a complaint to the IVG whose decision shall be conclusive.

c. The arrangements set forth in this clause shall be subject to review every ten years and may be altered or terminated by the agreement of both Parties.

10. Electromagnetic Sphere

Neither Party's use of the electromagnetic sphere may interfere with the other Party's use.

Annex X shall detail arrangements relating to the use of the electromagnetic sphere.

The IVG shall monitor and verify the implementation of this clause and Annex X.

Any Party may submit a complaint to the IVG whose decision shall be conclusive.

11. Law Enforcement

The Israeli and Palestinian law enforcement agencies shall cooperate in combating illicit drug trafficking, illegal trafficking in archaeological artifacts and objects of arts, cross-border crime including theft and fraud, organized crime, trafficking in women and minors, counterfeiting, pirate TV and radio stations, and other illegal activities.

12. International Border Crossings

The following arrangements shall apply to borders crossing between the states of Palestine and Jordan, the states of Palestine and Egypt, as well as airport and seaport entry points to the state of Palestine.

All border crossings shall be monitored by joint teams composed of members of the PSF and the MF. These teams shall prevent the entry into Palestine of any weapons, materials, or equipment that are in contravention of the provisions of this Agreement.

The MF representatives and the PSF will have, jointly and separately, the authority to block the entry into Palestine of any such items. If at any time a disagreement regarding the entrance of goods or materials arises between the PSF and the MF representatives, the PSF may bring the matter to the IVG, whose binding conclusions shall be rendered within 24 hours.

This arrangement shall be reviewed by the IVG after 5 years to determine its continuation, modification, or termination. Thereafter, the Palestinian party may request such a review on an annual basis.

In passenger terminals, for thirty months, Israel may maintain an unseen presence in a designated on-site facility, to be staffed by members of the MF and Israelis, utilizing appropriate technology. The Israeli side may request that the MF-PSF conduct further inspections and take appropriate action.

For the following two years, these arrangements will continue in a specially designated facility in Israel, utilizing appropriate technology. This shall not cause delays beyond the procedures outlined in this clause.

In cargo terminals, for thirty months, Israel may maintain an unseen presence in a designated on-site facility, to be staffed by members of the MF and Israelis, utilizing appropriate technology. The Israeli side may request that the MF-PSF conduct further inspections and take appropriate action. If the Israeli side is not satisfied by the MF-PSF action, it may demand that the cargo be detained pending a decision by an MF inspector. The MF inspector's decision shall be binding and final and shall be rendered within 12 hours of the Israeli complaint.

viii. For the following three years, these arrangements will continue from a specially designated facility in Israel, utilizing appropriate technology. This shall not cause delays beyond the timelines outlined in this clause.

A high-level trilateral committee composed of representatives of Palestine, Israel, and the IVG shall meet regularly to monitor the application of these procedures and correct any irregularities and may be convened on request.

The details of the above are set forth in Annex X.

13. Border Control

The PSF shall maintain border control as detailed in Annex X.

The MF shall monitor and verify the maintenance of border control by the PSF.

Article 6—Jerusalem

1. Religious and Cultural Significance

i. The Parties recognize the universal historic, religious, spiritual, and cultural significance of Jerusalem and its holiness enshrined in Judaism, Christianity, and Islam. In recognition of this status, the Parties reaffirm their commitment to safeguard the character, holiness, and freedom of worship in the city and to respect the existing division of administrative functions and traditional practices between different denominations.

ii. The Parties shall establish an interfaith body consisting of representatives of the three monotheistic faiths, to act as a consultative body to the Parties on matters related to the city's religious significance and to promote interreligious understanding and dialogue. The composition, procedures, and modalities for this body are set forth in Annex X.

2. Capital of Two States

The Parties shall have their mutually recognized capitals in the areas of Jerusalem under their respective sovereignty.

3. Sovereignty

Sovereignty in Jerusalem shall be in accordance with attached Map 2. This shall not prejudice nor be prejudiced by the arrangements set forth below.

4. Border Regime

The border regime shall be designed according to the provisions of Article 11, and taking into account the specific needs of Jerusalem (e.g., movement of tourists and intensity of border crossing use including provisions for Jerusalemites) and the provisions of this Article.

5. Al-Haram al-Sharif/Temple Mount (Compound)

i. International Group

a. An International Group, composed of the IVG and other parties to be agreed upon by the Parties, including members of the Organization of the Islamic Conference (OIC), shall hereby be established to monitor, verify, and assist in the implementation of this clause.

b. For this purpose, the International Group shall establish a Multinational Presence on the Compound, the composition, structure, mandate, and functions of which are set forth in Annex X.

c. The Multinational Presence shall have specialized detachments dealing with security and conservation. The Multinational Presence shall make periodic conservation and security reports to the International Group. These reports shall be made public.

d. The Multinational Presence shall strive to immediately resolve any problems arising and may refer any unresolved disputes to the International Group that will function in accordance with Article 16.

e. The Parties may at any time request clarifications or submit complaints to the International Group which shall be promptly investigated and acted upon.

f. The International Group shall draw up rules and regulations to maintain security on and conservation of the Compound. These shall include lists of the weapons and equipment permitted on the site.

ii. Regulations Regarding the Compound

a. In view of the sanctity of the Compound, and in light of the unique religious and cultural significance of the site to the Jewish people, there shall be no digging, excavation, or construction on the Compound, unless approved by the two Parties. Procedures for regular maintenance and emergency repairs on the Compound shall be established by the IG after consultation with the Parties.

b. The state of Palestine shall be responsible for maintaining the security of the Compound and for ensuring that it will not be used for any hostile acts against Israelis or Israeli areas. The only arms permitted on the Compound shall be those carried by the Palestinian security personnel and the security detachment of the Multinational Presence.

c. In light of the universal significance of the Compound, and subject to security considerations and to the need not to disrupt religious worship or decorum on the site as determined by the Waqf, visitors shall be allowed access to the site. This shall be without any discrimination and generally be in accordance with past practice.

iii. Transfer of Authority

a. At the end of the withdrawal period stipulated in Article 5/7, the state of Palestine shall assert sovereignty over the Compound.

b. The International Group and its subsidiary organs shall continue to exist and fulfill all the functions stipulated in this Article unless otherwise agreed by the two Parties.

6. The Wailing Wall

The Wailing Wall shall be under Israeli sovereignty.

7. The Old City

i. Significance of the Old City

a. The Parties view the Old City as one whole enjoying a unique character. The Parties agree that the preservation of this unique character together with safeguarding and promoting the welfare of the inhabitants should guide the administration of the Old City.

b. The Parties shall act in accordance with the UNESCO World Cultural Heritage List regulations, in which the Old City is a registered site.

ii. IVG Role in the Old City

a. Cultural Heritage

1. The IVG shall monitor and verify the preservation of cultural heritage in the Old City in accordance with the UNESCO World Cultural Heritage List rules. For this purpose, the IVG shall have free and unimpeded access to sites, documents, and information related to the performance of this function.

2. The IVG shall work in close coordination with the Old City Committee of the Jerusalem Coordination and Development Committee (JCDC), including in devising a restoration and preservation plan for the Old City.

b. Policing

1. The IVG shall establish an Old City Policing Unit (PU) to liaise with, coordinate between, and assist the Palestinian and Israeli police forces in the Old City, to defuse localized tensions and help resolve disputes, and to perform policing duties in locations specified in and according to operational procedures detailed in Annex X.
2. The PU shall periodically report to the IVG.

c. Either Party may submit complaints in relation to this clause to the IVG, which shall promptly act upon them in accordance with Article 16.

iii. Free Movement Within the Old City

Movement within the Old City shall be free and unimpeded subject to the provisions of this article and rules and regulations pertaining to the various holy sites.

iv. Entry into and Exit from the Old City

a. Entry and exit points into and from the Old City will be staffed by the authorities of the state under whose sovereignty the point falls, with the presence of PU members, unless otherwise specified.
b. With a view to facilitating movement into the Old City, each Party shall take such measures at the entry points in its territory as to ensure the preservation of security in the Old City. The PU shall monitor the operation of the entry points.
c. Citizens of either Party may not exit the Old City into the territory of the other Party unless they are in possession of the relevant documentation that entitles them to. Tourists may only exit the Old City into the territory of the Party which they posses valid authorization to enter.

v. Suspension, Termination, and Expansion

a. Either Party may suspend the arrangements set forth in Article 6/7/iii in cases of emergency for one week. The extension of such suspension for longer than a week shall be pursuant to consultation with the other

Party and the IVG at the Trilateral Committee established in Article 3/3.

b. This clause shall not apply to the arrangements set forth in Article 6/7/vi.

c. Three years after the transfer of authority over the Old City, the Parties shall review these arrangements. These arrangements may only be terminated by agreement of the Parties.

d. The Parties shall examine the possibility of expanding these arrangements beyond the Old City and may agree to such an expansion.

vi. Special Arrangements

a. Along the way outlined in Map X (from the Jaffa Gate to the Zion Gate) there will be permanent and guaranteed arrangements for Israelis regarding access, freedom of movement, and security, as set forth in Annex X.

1. The IVG shall be responsible for the implementation of these arrangements.

b. Without prejudice to Palestinian sovereignty, Israeli administration of the Citadel will be as outlined in Annex X.

vii. Color-Coding of the Old City

A visible color-coding scheme shall be used in the Old City to denote the sovereign areas of the respective Parties.

viii. Policing

a. An agreed number of Israeli police shall constitute the Israeli Old City police detachment and shall exercise responsibility for maintaining order and day-to-day policing functions in the area under Israeli sovereignty.

b. An agreed number of Palestinian police shall constitute the Palestinian Old City police detachment and shall exercise responsibility for maintaining order and day-to-day policing functions in the area under Palestinian sovereignty.

c. All members of the respective Israeli and Palestinian Old City police detachments shall undergo special training, including joint training exercises, to be administered by the PU.

d. A special Joint Situation Room, under the direction of the PU and incorporating members of the Israeli and Palestinian Old City police detachments, shall facilitate liaison on all relevant matters of policing and security in the Old City.

ix. Arms

No person shall be allowed to carry or possess arms in the Old City, with the exception of the Police Forces provided for in this Agreement. In addition, each Party may grant special written permission to carry or possess arms in areas under its sovereignty.

x. Intelligence and Security

a. The Parties shall establish intensive intelligence cooperation regarding the Old City, including the immediate sharing of threat information.
b. A trilateral committee composed of the two Parties and representatives of the United States shall be established to facilitate this cooperation.

8. Mount of Olives Cemetery

i. The area outlined in Map X (the Jewish Cemetery on the Mount of Olives) shall be under Israeli administration; Israeli law shall apply to persons using and procedures appertaining to this area in accordance with Annex X.

a. There shall be a designated road to provide free, unlimited, and unimpeded access to the Cemetery.

b. The IVG shall monitor the implementation of this clause.

c. This arrangement may only be terminated by the agreement of both Parties.

9. Special Cemetery Arrangements

Arrangements shall be established in the two cemeteries designated in Map X (Mount Zion Cemetery and the German Colony Cemetery), to facilitate and ensure the continuation of the current burial and visitation practices, including the facilitation of access.

10. The Western Wall Tunnel

i. The Western Wall Tunnel designated in Map X shall be under Israeli administration, including:

a. Unrestricted Israeli access and right to worship and conduct religious practices.

b. Responsibility for the preservation and maintenance of the site in accordance with this Agreement and without damaging structures above, under IVG supervision.

c. Israeli policing.

d. IVG monitoring.

e. The Northern Exit of the Tunnel shall only be used for exit and may only be closed in case of emergency as stipulated in Article 6/7.

ii. This arrangement may only be terminated by the agreement of both Parties.

11. Municipal Coordination

i. The two Jerusalem municipalities shall form a Jerusalem Co-ordination and Development Committee (JCDC) to oversee the cooperation and coordination between the Palestinian Jerusalem municipality and the Israeli Jerusalem municipality. The JCDC and its subcommittees shall be composed of an equal number of representatives from Palestine and Israel. Each side will appoint members of the JCDC and its subcommittees in accordance with its own modalities.

ii. The JCDC shall ensure that the coordination of infrastructure and services best serves the residents of Jerusalem and shall promote the economic development of the city to the benefit of all. The JCDC will act to encourage cross-community dialogue and reconciliation.

iii. The JCDC shall have the following subcommittees:

a. A Planning and Zoning Committee: to ensure agreed planning and zoning regulations in areas designated in Annex X.

b. A Hydro Infrastructure Committee: to handle matters relating to drinking water delivery, drainage, and wastewater collection and treatment.

c. A Transport Committee: to coordinate relevant connectedness and compatibility of the two road systems and other issues pertaining to transport.

d. An Environmental Committee: to deal with environmental issues affecting the quality of life in the city, including solid waste management.

e. An Economic and Development Committee: to formulate plans for economic development in areas of joint interest, including in the areas of transportation, seam line commercial cooperation, and tourism.

f. A Police and Emergency Services Committee: to coordinate measures for the maintenance of public order and crime prevention and the provision of emergency services.

g. An Old City Committee: to plan and closely coordinate the joint provision of the relevant municipal services and other functions stipulated in Article 6/7.

Other Committees as agreed in the JCDC.

12. Israeli Residency of Palestinian Jerusalemites

Palestinian Jerusalemites who currently are permanent residents of Israel shall lose this status upon the transfer of authority to Palestine of those areas in which they reside.

13. Transfer of Authority

The Parties will apply in certain socioeconomic spheres interim measures to ensure the agreed, expeditious, and orderly transfer of powers and obligations from Israel to Palestine. This shall be done in a manner that preserves the accumulated socioeconomic rights of the residents of East Jerusalem.

Article 7—Refugees

1. Significance of the Refugee Problem

i. The Parties recognize that, in the context of two independent states, Palestine and Israel, living side by side in peace, an agreed resolution of the refugee problem is necessary for achieving a just, comprehensive, and lasting peace between them.

ii. Such a resolution will also be central to stability building and development in the region.

2. UNGAR 194, UNSC Resolution 242, and the Arab Peace Initiative

i. The Parties recognize that UNGAR 194, UNSC Resolution 242, and the Arab Peace Initiative (Article 2/ii) concerning the rights of the Palestinian refugees represent the basis for resolving the refugee issue and agree that these rights are fulfilled according to Article 7 of this Agreement.

3. Compensation

i. Refugees shall be entitled to compensation for their refugeehood and for loss of property. This shall not prejudice or be prejudiced by the refugee's permanent place of residence.

ii. The Parties recognize the right of states that have hosted Palestinian refugees to remuneration.

4. Choice of Permanent Place of Residence (PPR)

The solution to the PPR aspect of the refugee problem shall entail an act of informed choice on the part of the refugee to be exercised in accordance with the options and modalities set forth in this Agreement. PPR options from which the refugees may choose shall be as follows:

i. The state of Palestine, in accordance with clause a below.

ii. Areas in Israel being transferred to Palestine in the land swap, following assumption of Palestinian sovereignty, in accordance with clause a below.

iii. Third countries, in accordance with clause b below.

iv. The state of Israel, in accordance with clause c below.

v. Present host countries, in accordance with clause d below.

   a. PPR options i and ii shall be the right of all Palestinian refugees and shall be in accordance with the laws of the state of Palestine.

   b. Option iii shall be at the sovereign discretion of third countries and shall be in accordance with numbers that each third country will submit to the International Commission. These numbers shall represent the total number of Palestinian refugees that each third country shall accept.

   c. Option iv shall be at the sovereign discretion of Israel and will be in accordance with a number that Israel will submit to the International Commission. This number shall represent the total number of Palestinian refugees that Israel shall accept. As a basis, Israel will consider the average of the total numbers submitted by the different third countries to the International Commission.

   d. Option v shall be in accordance with the sovereign discretion of present host countries. Where exercised this shall be in the context of prompt and extensive development and rehabilitation programs for the refugee communities.

Priority in all the above shall be accorded to the Palestinian refugee population in Lebanon.

5. Free and Informed Choice

The process by which Palestinian refugees shall express their PPR choice shall be on the basis of a free and informed decision. The Parties themselves are committed and will encourage third parties to facilitate the refugees' free choice in expressing their preferences and to countering any attempts at interference or organized pressure on the process of choice. This will not prejudice the recognition of Palestine as the realization of Palestinian self-determination and statehood.

6. End of Refugee Status

Palestinian refugee status shall be terminated upon the realization of an individual refugee's permanent place of residence (PPR) as determined by the International Commission.

7. End of Claims

This agreement provides for the permanent and complete resolution of the Palestinian refugee problem. No claims may be raised except for those related to the implementation of this Agreement.

8. International Role

The Parties call upon the international community to participate fully in the comprehensive resolution of the refugee problem in accordance with this Agreement, including, inter alia, the establishment of an International Commission and an International Fund.

9. Property Compensation

i. Refugees shall be compensated for the loss of property resulting from their displacement.
ii. The aggregate sum of property compensation shall be calculated as follows:

   a. The Parties shall request the International Commission to appoint a Panel of Experts to estimate the value of Palestinians' property at the time of displacement.

b. The Panel of Experts shall base its assessment on the UNCCP records, the records of the Custodian for Absentee Property, and any other records it deems relevant. The Parties shall make these records available to the Panel.

c. The Parties shall appoint experts to advise and assist the Panel in its work.

d. Within 6 months, the Panel shall submit its estimates to the Parties.

e. The Parties shall agree on an economic multiplier, to be applied to the estimates, to reach a fair aggregate value of the property.

iii. The aggregate value agreed to by the Parties shall constitute the Israeli "lump sum" contribution to the International Fund. No other financial claims arising from the Palestinian refugee problem may be raised against Israel.

iv. Israel's contribution shall be made in installments in accordance with Schedule X.

v. The value of the Israeli fixed assets that shall remain intact in former settlements and transferred to the state of Palestine will be deducted from Israel's contribution to the International Fund. An estimation of this value shall be made by the International Fund, taking into account assessment of damage caused by the settlements.

10. Compensation for Refugeehood

i. A "Refugeehood Fund" shall be established in recognition of each individual's refugeehood. The Fund, to which Israel shall be a contributing party, shall be overseen by the International Commission. The structure and financing of the Fund is set forth in Annex X.

ii. Funds will be disbursed to refugee communities in the former areas of UNRWA operation and will be at their disposal for communal development and commemoration of the refugee experience. Appropriate mechanisms will be devised by the International Commission whereby the beneficiary refugee communities are empowered to determine and administer the use of this Fund.

11. The International Commission (Commission)

i. Mandate and Composition

a. An International Commission shall be established and shall have full and exclusive responsibility for implementing all aspects of this Agreement pertaining to refugees.

b. In addition to themselves, the Parties call upon the United Nations, the United States, UNRWA, the Arab host countries, the European Union, Switzerland, Canada, Norway, Japan, the World Bank, the Russian Federation, and others to be the members of the Commission.

c. The Commission shall

1. Oversee and manage the process whereby the status and PPR of Palestinian refugees is determined and realized.
2. Oversee and manage, in close cooperation with the host states, the rehabilitation and development programs.
3. Raise and disburse funds as appropriate.

d. The Parties shall make available to the Commission all relevant documentary records and archival materials in their possession that it deems necessary for the functioning of the Commission and its organs. The Commission may request such materials from all other relevant parties and bodies, including, inter alia, UNCCP and UNRWA.

ii. Structure

a. The Commission shall be governed by an Executive Board (Board) composed of representatives of its members.

b. The Board shall be the highest authority in the Commission and shall make the relevant policy decisions in accordance with this Agreement.

c. The Board shall draw up the procedures governing the work of the Commission in accordance with this Agreement.

d. The Board shall oversee the conduct of the various Committees of the Commission. The said Committees shall periodically report to the Board in accordance with procedures set forth thereby.

e. The Board shall create a Secretariat and appoint a Chair thereof. The Chair and the Secretariat shall conduct the day-to-day operation of the Commission.

iii. Specific Committees

a. The Commission shall establish the Technical Committees specified below.

b. Unless otherwise specified in this Agreement, the Board shall determine the structure and procedures of the Committees.

c. The Parties may make submissions to the Committees as deemed necessary.

d. The Committees shall establish mechanisms for resolution of disputes arising from the interpretation or implementation of the provisions of this Agreement relating to refugees.

e. The Committees shall function in accordance with this Agreement and shall render binding decisions accordingly.

f. Refugees shall have the right to appeal decisions affecting them according to mechanisms established by this Agreement and detailed in Annex X.

iv. Status–determination Committee

a. The Status-determination Committee shall be responsible for verifying refugee status.

b. UNRWA registration shall be considered as rebuttable presumption (prima facie proof) of refugee status.

v. Compensation Committee

a. The Compensation Committee shall be responsible for administering the implementation of the compensation provisions.

b. The Committee shall disburse compensation for individual property pursuant to the following modalities:

1. Either a fixed per capita award for property claims below a specified value. This will require the claimant to only prove title and shall be processed according to a fast-track procedure, or

2. A claims-based award for property claims exceeding a specified value for immovables and other assets. This will require the claimant to prove both title and the value of the losses.

c. Annex X shall elaborate the details of the above including, but not limited to, evidentiary issues and the use of UNCCP, "Custodian for Absentees' Property," and UNRWA records, along with any other relevant records.

vi. Host State Remuneration Committee

There shall be remuneration for host states.

vii. Permanent Place of Residence Committee (PPR Committee)

The PPR Committee shall

a. Develop with all the relevant parties detailed programs regarding the implementation of the PPR options pursuant to Article 7/4 above.

b. Assist the applicants in making an informed choice regarding PPR options.

c. Receive applications from refugees regarding PPR. The applicants must indicate a number of preferences in accordance with article 7/4 above. The applications shall be received no later than two years after the start of the International Commission's operations. Refugees who do not submit such applications within the two-year period shall lose their refugee status.

d. Determine, in accordance with sub-Article (a) above, the PPR of the applicants, taking into account individual preferences and maintenance of family unity. Applicants who do not avail themselves of the Committee's PPR determination shall lose their refugee status.

e. Provide the applicants with the appropriate technical and legal assistance.

f. The PPR of Palestinian refugees shall be realized within 5 years of the start of the International Commission's operations.

viii. Refugeehood Fund Committee

The Refugeehood Fund Committee shall implement Article 7/10 as detailed in Annex X.

ix. Rehabilitation and Development Committee

In accordance with the aims of this Agreement and noting the above PPR programs, the Rehabilitation and Development Committee shall work closely with Palestine, Host Countries, and other relevant third countries and parties in pursuing the goal of refugee rehabilitation and community development. This shall include devising programs and plans to provide the former refugees with opportunities for personal and communal development, housing, education, healthcare, retraining, and other needs. This shall be integrated in the general development plans for the region.

12. The International Fund

i. An International Fund (the Fund) shall be established to receive contributions outlined in this Article and additional contributions from the international community. The Fund shall disburse monies to the Commission to enable it to carry out its functions. The Fund shall audit the Commission's work.

ii. The structure, composition, and operation of the Fund are set forth in Annex X.

13. UNRWA

i. UNRWA should be phased out in each country in which it operates, based on the end of refugee status in that country.

ii. UNRWA should cease to exist five years after the start of the Commission's operations. The Commission shall draw up a plan for the phasing out of UNRWA and shall facilitate the transfer of UNRWA functions to host states.

14. Reconciliation Programs

i. The Parties will encourage and promote the development of co-operation between their relevant institutions and civil societies in creating forums for exchanging historical narratives and enhancing mutual understanding regarding the past.

ii. The Parties shall encourage and facilitate exchanges in order to disseminate a richer appreciation of these respective narratives, in the fields of formal and informal education, by providing conditions for direct contacts between schools, educational institutions, and civil society.

iii. The Parties may consider cross-community cultural programs in order to promote the goals of conciliation in relation to their respective histories.

iv. These programs may include developing appropriate ways of commemorating those villages and communities that existed prior to 1949.

Article 8—Israeli-Palestinian Cooperation Committee (IPCC)

1. The Parties shall establish an Israeli-Palestinian Cooperation Committee immediately upon the entry into force of this Agreement. The IPCC shall be a ministerial-level body with ministerial-level Co-Chairs.

2. The IPCC shall develop and assist in the implementation of policies for cooperation in areas of common interest including, but not limited to, infrastructure needs, sustainable development and environmental issues, cross-border municipal cooperation, border area industrial parks, exchange programs, human resource development, sports and youth, science, agriculture, and culture.

3. The IPCC shall strive to broaden the spheres and scope of cooperation between the Parties.

Article 9—Designated Road Use Arrangements

1. The following arrangements for Israeli civilian use will apply to the designated roads in Palestine as detailed in Map X (Road 443, Jerusalem to Tiberias via Jordan Valley, and Jerusalem–Ein Gedi).
2. These arrangements shall not prejudice Palestinian jurisdiction over these roads, including PSF patrols.
3. The procedures for designated road use arrangements will be further detailed in Annex X.
4. Israelis may be granted permits for use of designated roads. Proof of authorization may be presented at entry points to the designated roads. The sides will review options for establishing a road use system based on smart card technology.
5. The designated roads will be patrolled by the MF at all times. The MF will establish with the states of Israel and Palestine agreed arrangements for cooperation in emergency medical evacuation of Israelis.
6. In the event of any incidents involving Israeli citizens and requiring criminal or legal proceedings, there will be full cooperation between the Israeli and the Palestinian authorities according to arrangements to be agreed upon as part of the legal cooperation between the two states. The Parties may call on the IVG to assist in this respect.
7. Israelis shall not use the designated roads as a means of entering Palestine without the relevant documentation and authorization.
8. In the event of regional peace, arrangements for Palestinian civilian use of designated roads in Israel shall be agreed and come into effect.

Article 10—Sites of Religious Significance

1. The Parties shall establish special arrangements to guarantee access to agreed sites of religious significance, as will be detailed in Annex X. These arrangements will apply, inter alia, to the Tomb of the Patriarchs in Hebron and Rachel's Tomb in Bethlehem, and Nabi Samuel.
2. Access to and from the sites will be by way of designated shuttle facilities from the relevant border crossing to the sites.
3. The Parties shall agree on requirements and procedures for granting licenses to authorized private shuttle operators.
4. The shuttles and passengers will be subject to MF inspection.
5. The shuttles will be escorted on their route between the border crossing and the sites by the MF.

6. The shuttles shall be under the traffic regulations and jurisdiction of the Party in whose territory they are traveling.

7. Arrangements for access to the sites on special days and holidays are detailed in Annex X.

8. The Palestinian Tourist Police and the MF will be present at these sites.

9. The Parties shall establish a joint body for the religious administration of these sites.

10. In the event of any incidents involving Israeli citizens and requiring criminal or legal proceedings, there will be full cooperation between the Israeli and the Palestinian authorities according to arrangements to be agreed upon. The Parties may call on the IVG to assist in this respect.

11. Israelis shall not use the shuttles as a means of entering Palestine without the relevant documentation and authorization.

12. The Parties shall protect and preserve the sites of religious significance listed in Annex X and shall facilitate visitation to the cemeteries listed in Annex X.

Article 11—Border Regime

1. There shall be a border regime between the two states, with movement between them subject to the domestic legal requirements of each and to the provisions of this Agreement as detailed in Annex X.

2. Movement across the border shall only be through designated border crossings.

3. Procedures in border crossings shall be designed to facilitate strong trade and economic ties, including labor movement between the Parties.

4. Each Party shall each, in its respective territory, take the measures it deems necessary to ensure that no persons, vehicles, or goods enter the territory of the other illegally.

5. Special border arrangements in Jerusalem shall be in accordance with Article 6 above.

Article 12—Water

Article 13—Economic Relations

Article 14—Legal Cooperation

These articles relate to professional matters that are being dealt with by teams of experts, upon completion of the work of these teams, they will be presented to the public.

Article 15—Palestinian Prisoners and Detainees

1. In the context of this Permanent Status Agreement between Israel and Palestine, the end of conflict, cessation of all violence, and the robust security arrangements set forth in this Agreement, all the Palestinian and Arab prisoners detained in the framework of the Israeli–Palestinian conflict prior to the date of signature of this Agreement, DD/MM/2003, shall be released in accordance with the categories set forth below and detailed in Annex X.

i. *Category A:* All persons imprisoned prior to the start of the implementation of the Declaration of Principles on May 4, 1994, administrative detainees, and minors, as well as women, and prisoners in ill health shall be released immediately upon the entry into force of this Agreement.

ii. *Category B:* All persons imprisoned after May 4, 1994, and prior to the signature of this Agreement shall be released no later than eighteen months from the entry into force of this Agreement, except those specified in Category C.

iii. *Category C:* Exceptional cases—persons whose names are set forth in Annex X—shall be released in thirty months at the end of the full implementation of the territorial aspects of this Agreement set forth in Article 5/7/v.

Article 16—Dispute Settlement Mechanism

1. Disputes related to the interpretation or application of this Agreement shall be resolved by negotiations within a bilateral framework to be convened by the High Steering Committee.
2. If a dispute is not settled promptly by the above, either Party may submit it to mediation and conciliation by the IVG mechanism in accordance with Article 3.
3. Disputes which cannot be settled by bilateral negotiation and/or the IVG mechanism shall be settled by a mechanism of conciliation to be agreed upon by the Parties.
4. Disputes which have not been resolved by the above may be submitted by either Party to an arbitration panel. Each Party shall nominate one

member of the three-member arbitration panel. The Parties shall select a third arbiter from the agreed list of arbiters set forth in Annex X either by consensus or, in the case of disagreement, by rotation.

Article 17—Final Clauses

Including a final clause providing for a UNSCR/UNGAR resolution endorsing the agreement and superseding the previous UN resolutions. The English version of this text will be considered authoritative.

INDEX

ABOUT THE AUTHOR

Dr. Moises F. Salinas was born in Mexico City, Mexico, in 1966. He has been involved in Israel-related activities from the age of 15 when he attended the Aluma Institute for Jewish Education, which was a program on Jewish education and leadership. He then served as a youth councilor in the Dor Hadash Organization, affiliated with the Hashomer Hatzair movement, in Mexico City. Later (1985–86), he served as Secretary General of the organization that had about 150 members and designed educational activities for youth aged 10–18.

Dr. Salinas first came to Israel in 1984–85 when he attended the Machon, the Institute for Youth Leaders From Abroad, in Jerusalem. He returned to Israel in 1986 to study at the Hebrew University, earning his BA in Educational Psychology (Cum Laude) in 1991. While studying, he worked and volunteered on a kibbutz as an adoptive student during weekends and vacations and worked in the Diaspora Museum and in several voluntary organizations in Jerusalem. He was an active participant of the Peace Now movement and a member of the Mapam (Meretz) party student wing.

Returning to Mexico City in 1991 to resume his studies, Dr. Salinas completed his MA in Psychology (he minored in Jewish Studies) in 1994. In 1998, he earned a Ph.D. in Educational Psychology from the University of Texas at Austin. Dr. Salinas then moved to Hartford, CT, where he continued his academic activities.

In 1999 he accepted a position as Assistant Professor of Psychology at Central Connecticut State University. His research focuses on the effects of stereotypes on academic performance and reducing the performance gap between minorities and nonminorities through learner-centered education. He has published a large number of articles and chapters in areas related to educational and social psychological issues. His first book,

The Politics of Stereotype: Psychology and Affirmative Action, was published by Greenwood-Praeger in 2003.

Dr. Salinas set out to open an American Zionist Movement branch for the Greater Hartford region. Since 2003, he serves as founding chairman of the Board and President pro tem. In this capacity, he strives to infuse the organization with a variety of pro-peace activities.

In 2004, Dr. Salinas became one of fourteen young Zionist leaders worldwide to be honored with the first Herzl Awards from the World Zionist Organization, in honor of the 100th anniversary of the death of Theodor Herzl, for his contributions to the Zionist Movement. He moved with his family to Israel during 2005–06 to work on the present book and developed close ties with several Israeli and Palestinian figures in the peace camp.